3 years of British Television

a.s. berman

cover & interior design
Pamela Norman

text ©2008 A.S. Berman

photography

Lenny Henry courtesy of Raymond Keith

John Inman courtesy of International Artistes

AYBS and Gorden Kaye courtesy of BBC

Eric Idle courtesy of ID Public Relations

John Mortimer by Julian Calder/Viking

Clive Swift courtesy of Roxane Vacca Mgt.

Blythe Duff courtesy of SMG Productions

Craig Charles & Robert Llewellyn by
Mike Vaughn ©Grant Naylor Productions Ltd.

Geraldine Somerville
courtesy of Granada Television

Beryl & Sue Vertue and **Coupling**
courtesy of Hartswood Films

Penelope Keith courtesy of
Burnett Granger Crowther LTD

Union jack ©Nic Taylor

Retro TV ©Marguerite Voisey

BearManor Media
P.O. Box 71426
Albany, GA 31708 USA
bearmanormedia.com

Printed by **Lightning Source**

Library of Congress
Cataloging-in-Publication Data

A.S Berman
30 Years of British Television
A.S. Berman, author.
  p.cm.
  Includes bibliographical references & index.
  ISBN 1-59393-143-3
1. British television, 1970-2000. 2. Biography.
3. British television—History. I. Title.

10 9 8 7 6 5 4 3 2 1

thanks

My thanks go to Ben Ohmart, the Papa Bear at BearManor Media, who gave these great voices of British television's past and present another chance to speak directly to their audiences.

I also would like to thank Rich and Judy Berman who have never stopped offering me love and encouragement, rooting for me no matter what crazy scheme I turned my hand to.

Thanks also go to *British Television* publisher Dan Abramson, who helped me bring that magazine to life and make it what it was.

Finally, I owe a debt of gratitude to my partner-in-crime and the love of my life. This book is for Pamela Norman, who never stopped believing in a brighter tomorrow, and made that tomorrow come true.

foreword

IT WAS SOMETHING OF A LIMITED WORLD for the
British television addict in the days before the World Wide Web took
hold. Sure, you could get your weekly fix of British comedy and drama
on your local PBS station, and the occasional Anglo offering cropped
up on the A&E and Comedy Central cable channels as each struggled
to find its respective identity. Yet, if you were an American who wanted
to find out anything at all about the people with the funny accents
who regularly delighted you on *Are You Being Served* or the plethora
of mystery series that sprouted like mushrooms every year, there
was little you could do short of taking out a prohibitively expensive
subscription to the UK's *Radio Times* magazine.

In the Spring of 1995, Dan Abramson and I published the first issue
of *British Television*, a quarterly magazine that sought to introduce
American audiences to the stars of that much-loved medium through a
series of in-depth interviews.

A year or so before, Dan and his business partner, Larry Jaffee, had
brought me on board another publication, *The Walford Gazette*, to write
for and layout that tabloid about the legendary British soap *EastEnders*
— my first paid writing job. But Dan and I both found ourselves
wanting to discuss other great British programs in print, and decided
a magazine was the way to go. Dan elected to write some articles and
handle the business end of things from his home in Queens as *British
Television's* publisher, and I signed on as writer, editor and layout person
in my native Northern Virginia.

The next three years were a blur of deadlines, learning by trial and
error how to produce a 20-page magazine on a tiny Macintosh Classic

(and with a local printer who had never printed a magazine before), and navigating the ordered tedium that is bulk-mail sortation. But that time was also peppered with glittering conversations with such British telly luminaries as John Inman, Lenny Henry, Penelope Keith and others who turned out to be as charming and magnanimous as every fan suspected them to be. This often baffled me when I, in my early 20s at the time, found myself in my dimly-lit home production area chatting away with actors and actresses who were larger stars in my world than the hottest box office draws are in the world at large.

Early on I explained our ability to speak with these people as a consequence of their inability to know just how small our magazine was. "All they know is an American magazine is calling, and they are only too happy to respond," I remember saying at the time. *(Cringe.)* However, I soon outgrew this American-centric mindset, realizing instead that their willingness to speak with us had less to do with our status as citizens of the US and more with their own humility. Over and over I was left with the impression that each actor saw his or her job as just that, a job, and all were perfectly willing to candidly discuss the ups and downs of the profession.

What follows are interviews culled from my personal telephone conversations with those individuals between 1995 and 1998, as well as a recent talk with producers Beryl and Sue Vertue. I only wish that Dan could've seen the book you now hold in your hands. He passed away in 1999 from colon cancer at the age of 45.

A.S.B.
Loveland, Colo.
April 2008

contents

the '70s   the '80s

the '90s

the '00s & beyond

introduction

THERE EXISTS IN AMERICA a club as little understood as
the Freemasons, complete with its own arcane language, rituals and
fashions. And like that ancient order its members walk among us,
perfectly normal individuals, until you get them in a room together
and someone intones any one of a number of secret handshake
phrases:

"Are you free, Mr. Humphries? I'm free!"
"The Bouquet residence, the lady of the house speaking!"
"No one expects the Spanish Inquisition!"

Since the Public Broadcasting Service first climbed onto the
airwaves in 1970, American audiences have been exposed to some
of the best comedies, dramas and mysteries Great Britain has to offer
— quality alternatives to whatever lowest-common-denominator
entertainment dominated the networks at any given time. Since cable
television joined the fray in the 1980s, even more British television has
made the rounds Stateside.

More recently, American audiences have been faced with a virtually
limitless supply of British programming thanks to several innovations,
including reasonably-priced "region free" DVD players that enable
those outside the UK to watch UK-only discs, and the increasing
penetration of the BBC America cable channel in the US.

While today's British telly connoisseurs are discovering the likes
of *Little Britain*, *The Catherine Tate Show* and the new *Doctor Who*, many
die-hard fans in North America still look back at the years between
1970 and 2000 with a glimmer of nostalgia.

The Golden Age of British Television

Before there was very much available on home video, one usually
had the opportunity to see a Britcom only as part of a weekly block of
programming on the local PBS station, making every viewing a treat.
In the '70s and '80s, the absurd insanity of *Monty Python's Flying Circus*
(page 17) was a much-loved mainstay, as were the Penelope Keith (page
45) classics *The Good Neighbors* and *To the Manor Born.* Then there was
the dramatic comedy (or is that comedic drama?) *Rumpole of the Bailey*
created by writer-barrister John Mortimer (page 25), whose barrister
Horace Rumpole (Leo McKern) habitually cut through the hypocrisy of
human dealings with an elegiac tone and a line or two of Wordsworth
to sweeten the disillusionment.

Later, the double entendre tour de force *Are You Being Served* and its
tales of life and love in the fictional Grace Brothers department store
developed such a rampant following in the States, its stars, including
John Inman (page 35), were frequently flown to the US to drum up
viewer support during PBS pledge drives, decades after the series had
ended. (The *Are You Being Served* zaniness lived on in another sitcom
written by the same scribes. *'Allo, 'Allo,* set in occupied France during
World War II, starred Gorden Kaye (page 59) as café owner René Artois.)

In the 1990s, the crown was passed to a series that was easily as
polarizing at the time as politics are today, on grounds of humor rather
than social policy. If you spent any time at all watching Britcoms,
you either loved *Keeping Up Appearances* or you changed the channel
the moment you saw that feather duster flit across the stack of books
on the screen. Week after week you watched Hyacinth Bucket ("it's
pronounced *Bouquet*") — played by Patricia Routledge — resort to
outrageous extremes to climb the social ladder, only to have fate and
her family, including long-suffering husband Richard, played by Clive
Swift (page 99), yank her back down to Earth.

The '90s continued to be a watershed decade for comedy with
Waiting For God, which offered up one of the most unlikely settings
for a sitcom ever: a Bournemouth retirement home. Within its walls,

retired photojournalist Diana Trent, played to the curmudgeonly hilt by Stephanie Cole (page 89), and dotty Tom Ballard (Graham Crowden) rallied their fellow "inmates" against the penny-pinching machinations of Bayview Retirement Village head Harvey Nigel Bains (Daniel Hill) for four years.

It was also in the '90s that the A&E cable channel, still struggling to find its niche, began to import so many British mystery series that it seemed to be trying to corner the market. In a way, it was. While PBS was still airing the "quaint" mysteries of the *Poirot* and *Inspector Morse* variety, A&E, perhaps in an attempt to match the grittiness of its true crime programs, was bringing out the big guns. Every Tuesday night it unearthed a new British series, from *A Touch of Frost* with David Jason as a renegade police detective to *Silent Witness*, which regularly saw pathologist Dr. Sam Ryan (Amanda Burton) carving up a corpse or three every episode to discover a murderer's identity, years before *CSI* made such things a daily event. However, it was with the airing of the Granada Television series *Cracker* that it introduced American audiences to a caliber of drama that has yet to be surpassed.

On paper it doesn't sound like much. Criminal psychologist Eddie "Fitz" Fitzgerald (the titular "cracker"), plagued by addictions to gambling, drink and cigarettes, only feels truly alive when he's helping the cops catch the murderers that plague Manchester. Two things made this a standout show. First were the formidable acting talents of Robbie Coltrane as Fitz, Geraldine Somerville (page 133) as Detective Sergeant Jane Penhaligon, and a cavalcade of stellar performers. Then there were the scripts by Jimmy McGovern that delved deeply into the lives of the show's characters and examined the gray areas of the human experience. The series quickly became one of the best in the history of not just British television, but English-language television overall.

Although the PBS offering *Taggart* lacks the psychological nuances of *Cracker*, the long-running Scottish police series (1983

– present) excels at concocting bizarre crimes for its investigators to solve. Even more compelling is the fact that *Taggart* has persevered despite the 1994 death of Mark McManus, the actor who portrayed the title character, Det. Chief Inspector Jim Taggart. (Blythe Duff, page 65, who plays police detective Jackie Reid, became the longest serving cast member on the show in 2001.)

While all this was going on, the BBC unleashed one of those bizarre comedies that it likes to put out there from time to time to prove that it isn't nearly as stuffy as people think it is. *Red Dwarf* began with Dave Lister (played with a befuddled charm by Craig Charles, page 75), a technician assigned to the mining spaceship Red Dwarf, revived from suspended animation after 3 million years to find himself the last human being in the universe. His only companions are crew member Arnold Rimmer (Chris Barrie), brought back to life as a hologram by the ship's computer, Holly, to keep Lister from cracking up; and Cat (Danny John-Jules), a man-cat creature that evolved from Lister's pregnant kitty, Frankenstein, which survived in the ship's hold. Later this motley crew picked up a new member in the form of Robert Llewellyn's Kryten (page 75), a wise, and at times subtly snarky, servant robot.

A bit more down-to-Earth, *Chef* popped up on many PBS schedules during the 1990s, giving the lovable comedic actor Lenny Henry (page 113) the opportunity to fuss and fume as the gastronomic genius Gareth Blackstock.

2000 and Beyond

By the year 2000, British television had gained several new footholds in the United States. While PBS stations continued to showcase many of the comedies from the golden age (and do so to this day), a great deal had changed.

Before, British programs that aired in the U.S. were like beams of light from a faraway star — by the time they made it across the Atlantic, they were several years old. Now, some Americans could subscribe to the BBC America cable channel, and many others were buying DVDs of current shows released in the UK. While British television remained a treat for American audiences who went for that sort of thing, the programs no longer had that feel of being the fruits of a membership in a secret society.

This is not to say that the quality of programming had in any way deteriorated. While this new availability of content exposed Americans to much more of Great Britain's lowest-common-denominator television, it also introduced them to more cutting-edge material. As it happens, much of it originated from a single production house: Hartswood Films. Case in point, the company, under the control of legendary television producer Beryl Vertue and her daughter Sue (page 145), took the done-to-death premise of thirtysomethings hanging out and falling in love and spun it into the hugely successful *Coupling*. Thanks to the brilliant television writer Steven Moffat (who also happens to be married to Sue Vertue), the series employed innovative time lines, insightful dialogue and insane situations to address the absurdities of, well, coupling. And the Hartswood production *Jekyll*, also penned by Moffat, reinvigorated Robert Louis Stevenson's classic tale for the modern age.

Yes, the new millennium of British television is off to an impressive start. Still, for many of us, those 30 years of British television always will remain a time when partaking of a gentle comedy or a gripping mystery wasn't simply a question of pulling a DVD off a shelf, but something more akin to a unifying experience. Just by switching on our televisions we were able to visit with our old friends at Grace Brothers or Bayview. And we also knew that at that precise moment, many other likeminded souls were doing precisely the same thing.

eric idle

Do Not Adjust Your Set

Monty Python's Flying Circus

IT IS VIRTUALLY IMPOSSIBLE to exaggerate the importance of Monty Python when discussing the spread of British television in the United States. Ironically, it was this troupe of six Ivy-League educated Britons who democratized British television for the masses.

With the 1969 launch of their landmark BBC program, *Monty Python's Flying Circus*, Graham Chapman, Eric Idle, John Cleese, Terry Jones, Michael Palin and Terry Gilliam poked fun at obscure subjects such as Marcel Proust's epic series *A la recherche du temps perdu* and Icelandic sagas as often as they resorted to "silly walks" and jaunty ditties about lumberjacks. While it never was their intention to send viewers scurrying to the local library in order to understand a gag, the Pythons did exactly that. In the process, they prepared audiences everywhere — Americans especially — for future British television such as *Blackadder* and other programs that dabble extensively in the minutiae of history.

Much has been written about Monty Python over the years, and for good reason. Together and individually every member of the group has accomplished a great deal. Before his death in 1989, Graham Chapman was a member of the Dangerous Sports Club; Gilliam has become a well-regarded director; Cleese has a species of lemur named

It should be noted that Chapman did not die as a result of these "dangerous sports" but succumbed to a rare form of spinal cancer.

after him; travel documentary maker Palin has two British *trains* named after him; and Terry Jones has become a renowned historian.

Then there is Eric Idle. He more than any of his fellow Pythons has stayed squarely in the humor game. He's co-written the music and lyrics for the musical *Monty Python's Spamalot*, penned at least half a dozen books, lent his voice to three episodes of *The Simpsons* and Merlin in *Shrek the Third*.

Born March 29, 1943, in what is now Tyne and Wear, England, Idle was quickly introduced to the harshness of life, losing his father in a traffic accident when he was 2. By 7 he was enrolled as a boarder in the Royal Wolverhampton School. By keeping his head down and studying away, he eventually landed himself a spot at Pembroke College at the University of Cambridge. There Idle joined the famous Footlights amateur dramatics group, where he met Cleese and Chapman. It was while performing in the Footlights Review at the Edinburgh Festival that he met Palin and Jones who were appearing in the Oxford Review. In 1967, Idle joined those two on the TV series *Do Not Adjust Your Set*, where he met Gilliam.

What the sextet subsequently did with the television show *Monty Python's Flying Circus* is still being appreciated, analyzed, quoted, misquoted and deified today. When I had the chance to exchange e-mails with Idle in 1996, I was expecting an audience with a somewhat blasé individual reflecting the inevitable wearing on the nerves that comes with being a worldwide phenomenon for nearly 30 years. What I discovered instead were the thoughtful musings of a well-read individual with no fears about speaking his mind and, like several others in these pages, one far more concerned about the plight of his fellow human beings than anything else. Like happening upon the works of Monty Python, it was a refreshing discovery indeed.

Interview originally published in
British Television No. 6 | 1996

One of Monty Python's greatest achievements was the way it compelled its audience to study history and literature in order to understand some of the troupe's more esoteric references. Were there any members of Python who argued for the removal of material that your average person might not understand?

No. We have always used ourselves as the litmus test on what is funny. If we liked it, it was in. If not, not. One of the banes of executive development is the constant refrain, "Oh, we understand it and think it's funny, but will the average man in the street?" In my experience, the average person is far brighter and more intelligent than executives give them credit for. It is one of the causes of the constant trivialization of TV. Of course this becomes a self-fulfilling prophecy if you're not careful. But we always hated talking down to the audience.

Being one of the founders of the "Oxbridge School of Comedy," do you find anything entertaining in the rival "Manchester School" (e.g., The Comic Strip, French & Saunders, etc.)?

I always hate these "school of comedy" clichés. Usually they don't stand up to close examination. Since this is a club and a kind of school of comedy, there is some justification to identifying members of it. Cambridge has a tradition: Jonathan Miller, Peter Cook, Cleese, Idle, Chapman, Fry & Laurie, Rowan Atkinson, etc., etc. So does Oxford. In fact, there is a good stream of comedians from lots of other universities, e.g., Bristol.

Beyond the Fringe was a comedy stage show written by Peter Cook, Dudley Moore, Alan Bennett and Jonathan Miller in the 1960s, and is held by many to be the genesis of the Monty Python-style humor that pervaded the '70s and beyond.

Who influenced your comedy?

Well now, let's see. I guess you mean who did I like growing up. Tony Hancock, Bilko, Dick van Dyke, Round the Horne, Morecambe and Wise, Dick Emery, Jimmy Edwards, Frankie Howerd, Peter Sellers, Spike Milligan. My biggest influence was *Beyond the Fringe*. It changed my life. After that, the Cleese generation of Cambridge Circus showed me it was possible to actually do this kind of comedy.

In the book **Life of Python**, George Perry credits you with the introduction of women into the Footlights, and goes on to state that one of the young women was none other than celebrated feminist author Germaine Greer.

Keen-eyed viewers also will remember Greer's brief appearance in the **Absolutely Fabulous** episode "Hospital" in a dream sequence as Edina's mother.

Germaine was really funny. She came direct from Melbourne or Sydney University where she also did revue. Her audition piece was a nun doing a striptease! At the end of it, she put flippers on her feet and waddled off for a swim.

Do you think working with yourself and the rest of the Footlights crew set her on her more serious path of feminism and the writing of **The Female Eunuch**?

The Cambridge University Footlights Dramatic Club alumni include everyone from Monty Python's John Cleese, Graham Chapman and, of course, Eric Idle, to **Jeeves & Wooster's** Stephen Fry and Hugh Laurie, and **Keeping Up Appearances'** Clive Swift (see p. 99).

Well, she toured the UK with me in 1965 in a revue called *My Girl Herbert*, which sounds more like a male eunuch. She was bright and funny and very fond of men. In fact, she bet me she could bed every single member of the company. I took the bet, but she got stuck on the horn player in the band. She was a very fine actress and performer. Her humor is lethal.

66 Comedy is a young person's game. You have more moral certainties when you are young. Also, there are always younger people coming up behind. Frankly, I am tired of making comedy films. 99

Why did Britain lose the empire, and has it made a bit of difference? Do you think the BBC was somehow to blame?

Gosh! Erm. I think the Empire was lost before the BBC! Empires rise and fall. I think the fact that a tiny group of islands were able to stop fighting each other long enough to take the world shows what can be done when people cooperate. I am saddened to see this process in reverse. Where would we be without the Irish, the Scots and the Welsh? But we seem to be going backwards into the bickering and ultimate tribal warfare from whence we arose. I feel we should be proud of renouncing the Empire — there are many splendid achievements: cricket, some sense of parliamentary democracy, literature, the idea of fair play. Also by and large, the Empire was handed back to people without bloodshed. These are things we should be proud of. Instead of which we beat our breasts and allow other cultures to point to us as racist, domineering bastards, whereas we were in fact the first to renounce slavery — long before America. But unpleasant truths are rarely allowed to intrude in the States, which is, of course, the new Empire. Or was Hawaii always American? Oh, and Alaska and Puerto Rico.... Of course, as you know, the real reason for Empire is the British weather. A bunch of British pirates would land on some sunny shore and think, "Shall we sail back? Nah, let's just stop here."

So many people known for their humor have gone the serious route in the last few years: Robbie Coltrane, David Jason, Michael Palin, etc. Why do you think this is so, and do you see yourself abandoning humor for drama or documentary in the near future?

Comedy is a young person's game. You have more moral certainties when you are young. Also, there are always younger people coming up behind. Frankly, I am tired of making comedy films. I enjoyed playing Ratty (in *The Wind in the Willows*) precisely because he is a well-rounded character, without having to go for the laugh all the time. I can certainly see the appeal. I am not tempted into documentary. I like writing.

Where do you think you are more greatly appreciated: North America or Great Britain?

Oh, probably the States. In the UK we are great at greeting new talent and we are the first to despise the old. This is both good and bad. It means we do foster talent tremendously, but then we often don't know what to do with it. I suppose we are the same with our inventions. It is something to do with our ambivalence about success.

My final thought is that it is important to remember that life is more important than showbiz! You only get one life. At least so far as I know.

john mortimer

Rumpole of
the Bailey
Summer's Lease

IT IS A TALENTED WRITER indeed who can make audiences the world over fall in love with a member of the bar. But that's just what author John Mortimer has done for more than 30 years with his claret-swilling, poetry spouting, cheroot smoking barrister Horace Rumpole, haunter of that bastion of British justice, the Old Bailey.

Born April 21, 1923 in Hampstead, London, the Oxford-educated Mortimer started his own law career in 1948. During his time at the bar, Mortimer appeared as defense council in several high-profile cases including obscenity proceedings against the satirical magazine *Oz* in 1971, and for the Sex Pistols and Virgin Records in 1977 — a case that revolved around the use of the word "bollocks" in the punk band's famous album, *Never Mind the Bollocks, Here's the Sex Pistols*.

In 1975, after writing several novels, radio, stage and television plays, Mortimer turned his talents to drafting a one-off story for the BBC's TV anthology series, *Play For Today*. The tale, starring Australian-born actor Leo McKern, marked the debut of that Old Bailey hack and champion of London's criminal classes, Horace Rumpole.

Producer Irene Shubik approached BBC Head of Plays Christopher Morahan about having Mortimer write a further six episodes for a *Rumpole* series. While Morahan was all in favor of it, he soon left his position, and his replacement was not at all keen on the idea. Knowing she was on to a good thing, Shubik left the BBC, took the idea to Thames Television, and produced the first season of *Rumpole of the Bailey.*

The series debuted in 1978 with Julian Curry as Claude Erskine-Brown, Patricia Hodge as Phyllida "Portia" Trant and Peter Bowles as head of chambers Guthrie Featherstone — a cast that would continue on throughout the program's seven season run. Rumpole's wife, Hilda (known to Rumpole as "She Who Must Be Obeyed"), was played by Peggy Thorpe-Bates in Seasons 1, 2 and 3. Marion Mathie took over the role for the rest of the series.

Since *Rumpole's* debut, Mortimer has adapted the barrister's legal romps into a long-running series of books. Even after the series ended in 1992, original Rumpole novels and short story collections continue to appear on bookstore shelves as of this writing.

The author, who seldom makes international headlines, did so in February 2008: as an alibi to a murder charge. More accurately, as an alibi to one of many accusations made by Harrods owner Mohamed Al Fayed during the inquest into the 1997 death of Princess Diana and Al Fayed's son, Dodi.

Lord Fellowes, the Queen's former private secretary and husband of Diana's sister, Jane, was confronted with the entrepreneur's allegations that he had been involved in the death of his sister-in-law and Dodi in the infamous Paris car crash. Lord Fellowes denied being in Paris at the time of her death, saying that he was in a Norfolk church hall listening to a talk given by Mortimer on the night in question.

Had this happened to any other person, this event would likely disappear in a few days time, going the way of all items in today's 24/7 news culture. However, it would behoove Mr. Al Fayed and Lord Fellowes to heed the little confidence Mortimer revealed in the interview that follows. When a judge he appeared before as a barrister "was very stupid, I would put him into the next *Rumpole.*" Gentlemen, you've been warned.

> The exception to this came in 2004 when he met Ross Bentley, a son he never knew he had, the result of a once secret relationship with English actress Wendy Craig **(Butterflies, Not in Front of the Children).**

Interview originally published in
British Television No. 5 | 1996

Why did you choose a career at the bar?

I didn't choose it at all. I just wanted to be a writer, but my father said, "Just think of the awful lives that writers' wives have. Writers are always at home, you know. So get a job that gets you out of the house — divorce a few people." He said the work wasn't very difficult. The law was my way of making money until I was famous, like those who want to be film stars get jobs as waitresses.

Americans are pretty unabashed when it comes to expressing disapproval of lawyers as a group. Are they similarly sneered at in the United Kingdom?

Lawyers have always been the most unpopular people. We lived in the Temple, which is where all the barristers' chambers are. I think the barristers in England were rather respected in a way; it's a very gentlemanly profession. I don't think they've been as hated as American lawyers. I think every fourth American is a lawyer of some sort, whereas in England there aren't so many of them. There are only a very few barristers: three or four thousand. Of course I think one of the reasons lawyers like Rumpole is that he is a noble barrister.

Until Rumpole's debut in the 1970s, the only British legal fiction that had even flirted with fame was the Brothers in Law series by Henry Cecil. Were you at all influenced by his work?

Well, I wasn't. [Laughs.] I knew him, he was a judge — an impossible judge. He sort of came to decisions in court because he thought it was funny. Which was quite amusing for him, but not very nice for the people involved in the case.

Judge Henry Cecil Leon wrote comic tales of the English legal system in the '50s, '60s and '70s. His novel **Brothers in Law** became a TV series starring Richard Briers.

He sounds a bit like the judges that Rumpole regularly appears before, though most of those are depicted as extremely silly and heartless. Has this been your experience of judges?

The judges always come and say, "Why is it all the judges in *Rumpole* are always malignant or twits or malignant twits?" And I say, "Well, it's the Greek theory of drama, you know, because drama depends on conflict, and you can't have Rumpole standing up and the judge saying, 'OK, your client can go free.'" So the judge has to be nasty, really. The worst thing you can have is a totally fair judge, and then everybody gets convicted. But luckily there aren't very many of those about.

How much influence have you had over the televised interpretations of Rumpole?

I used to be able to approve the casting and nobody ever changed a line. I lived through the golden age of English television, which is rapidly declining. Towards the end of it, I had a television company of my own: New Penny Productions. We did the last *Rumpole* and some others. And it was my company so I didn't have any problem, really. But tell that to an American television writer and they're absolutely astonished.

And having so much influence, you've gone and inserted yourself into several episodes of the series, haven't you?

That was my idea. I do the Hitchcockian thing. I did that dinner scene in "Rumpole on Trial" and it seemed to take longer to say, "Pass the Madeira" — which was my one line — than it did to write the whole thing. You discover how actors are treated, which is terrible, because no one ever tells them what's going on, and you stand about miserably.

Rumpole very nearly was called something other than Rumpole, wasn't he?

I was in the Old Bailey defending some football hooligans with a rather sweet old barrister. These hooligans had tried to murder a supporter from the other team but they couldn't find any, so they just killed someone at Paddington Station one night. This barrister said — and this is the one who started the "old darling" thing — "I'm an anarchist at heart, but I don't even think my darling old Prince Peter Kropotkin would've approved of this."

Peter Kropotkin being a famous early Russian anarchist. So that's what we called it first: *My Darling Old Prince Peter Kropotkin.* But then of course the BBC said, "No one will have ever heard of Prince Peter Kropotkin." So I said, "Let's call it *My Darling Old Jean-Jacques Rousseau.*" And then they said they won't have heard of Jean-Jacques Rousseau, either. We called it *Rumpole of the Bailey.* He had another name, and then I found there was another barrister with this other name. So I thought Rumpole. I don't really know why, but everyone says it sounds very, very rude. I never meant it to be rude, it just came off the top of my head.

> "Old darling" is a term of (occasionally contemptuous) endearment used by Horace Rumpole in the series.

It's never been very clear to me which comes into creation first: the short stories or the television scripts.

Usually the *Rumpole* books have been adaptations of the scripts rather than the other way around.

Except for the last couple of books?

Yes, which is why perhaps they've been a bit better than the others.

Did the judges you appeared before treat you any better once they learned you were behind the Rumpole television series?

I remember I was making a speech, a passionate speech to a jury, and this judge suddenly interrupted me and said to the jury, "It may come as a relief for you to know that..." In the middle of this very sordid case he gave them the cricket score! And I thought that was the most awful thing to do, so I made Judge Bullingham in the next *Rumpole* do that. The judge came to me and said, "That's very unfair. I was watching *Rumpole* with my wife and we were looking forward to it and I heard this remark I made to you. Am I meant to be Judge Bullingham?" And I said, "How could anybody think that a kind, courteous person like you could be this old bastard?" He went off more or less satisfied. It didn't really make much difference. I had juries who used to convict my client and then come and ask me to sign copies of their book.

Of course you got a little of your own back with the power of the pen, and the television.
It was quite nice because, when the judge was very stupid, I would put him into the next *Rumpole*.

I understand you hung up the horsehair wig in the 1980s.
I didn't want to go on. I thought I would've left about 10 years earlier than I did. I knew I'd just be doing the same thing over and over again unless I wanted to be a judge, and I knew I didn't want to be a judge. I was doing this case in Singapore, defending this opposition MP, and I had dinner with *The Times* correspondent. I said, "I'm terribly tired and I've got all this responsibility and this man's whole future is in my hands. Why do I need it? I can make enough money writing to live on." The next morning, it said in *The Times* that I was going to give up being a lawyer, and I thought, "Well, if it says that in *The Times*, it must be true." So I gave it up.

Before you left the bar, however, you did something that would've made Rumpole himself groan with displeasure. You "took silk" and became a Queen's Council.

I enjoyed it much more. It's like going first class on the aeroplane instead of business class. You've got someone to do all the hard work for you, look up all the law — you don't need to know any law anymore. I never did know much.

Did you ever think Rumpole would find a home in the US?

Not at all. It is incredibly English. And after we'd done one series someone said it was on in Boston. Now it's more popular in America, really.

It's not being shown in the UK anymore, is it?

We've shown them all now and we don't repeat them very much. In England, it's terribly expensive to repeat shows because we have to pay all the actors again.

You've worked with most of the big TV production companies over the years. Are the independents any less bureaucratic than the BBC?

Well, you know there has been a terrible change in British television — one of Mrs. Thatcher's brilliant ideas. There is now a central scheduler, and this one man decides everything that's going to go on commercial television. None of these companies can decide what to show on television. Granada, Thames — well Thames doesn't exist anymore. They have to submit a script and a budget to this one bureaucrat, and he says whether they can do it. It's like having a central publisher who every publisher would have to submit a book to in order to see whether they could publish it. As it's turned out, it's become a nightmare, really, which is why I've avoided television for

❝ I had juries who used to convict my client and then come and ask me to sign copies of their book. ❞

awhile. So I would go to Thames and say, "I would like to do a *Rumpole* series" in the old days and they would say absolutely fine, here's the money, write the script sometime. And I would, and sometimes I wouldn't have written all the scripts before we'd started. Now you have to write all the scripts, tell him the cast (to this central chap), and he would then say, "I don't think I want it," so it's all become very unattractive.

Does that mean the BBC is looking better now?
The BBC would be better, but that is full of bureaucrats. The BBC is better in a way. Things creep through: *French & Saunders* and *Absolutely Fabulous*... The one good thing is Channel 4, which is outside all those and has produced these wonderful things like *The Madness of King George* and all these great movies, and *Four Weddings and a Funeral* — really good television.

Speaking of really good television, you adapted Evelyn Waugh's novel, Brideshead Revisited, for television. An able wordsmith yourself, one would imagine it might be tempting to improve on this classic.
No, I decided to keep it exactly like the book, and in a way you can do that much more in 11 hours of television than you can in a two-hour film. Writing an adaptation is like carpentry, really.

In 1982, a television adaptation of your stageplay A Voyage Round My Father aired.

What was that about?

My father went blind and I wrote a play about him. My mother was
alive when the play first came on, and she thought it was awful. She
thought it was terribly vulgar to write about your family. It was like
having a swimming pool or something like that. It was something you
didn't do. She died about the time it came on the stage.

You've just returned from a two-month tour of the States promoting your new book **Rumpole and the Angel of Death**. I understand in March you were in California addressing two chapters of the Rumpole Society.

I went to the one in San Francisco, which is very big, and we had a
lunch with about 250 people. Then I went to the Rumpole Society of
Los Angeles, had another 250 people, so they're very strong on the
West Coast.

One of the San Francisco group's main attractions is a replica of Rumpole's watering hole, Pommeroy's Wine Bar. Did you get to see it?

The first time I was there, they sort of built it in the Pacific Gas and
Electricity building. But I mean I have this odd effect on San Francisco
because when I did *Brideshead* they had Lord Sebastian look-alike
contests, and all the young men were carrying their Teddy bears down to
the marina. Now they have Hilda [Rumpole's wife] look-alike contests.

Did you enjoy your time in the States?

I did have a really good time. I went to Salt Lake City, which I'd never
been to before. I found it very nice, a really lovely, beautiful place. I told
a very rude story there, which was that the American test of obscenity
is what gave Mr. [Chief] Justice Rehnquist an erection. And afterwards
a woman came up to me and said, "Oh thank you so much. No one
would've mentioned an erection in Salt Lake City before."

john inman

Are You Being Served

Odd Man Out

WHILE HUNDREDS OF FACES have come and gone in the past few decades of British television, the gap-toothed grin of John Inman continues to be the one that symbolizes the medium's wit and whimsy for many viewers on this side of the Atlantic.

Born Frederick John Inman on June 28, 1935 in Preston, Lancashire, the actor won the hearts of millions the world over as the effeminate gentleman's counter assistant Mr. Humphries on the long-running BBC sitcom *Are You Being Served.*

At 13 Inman made his stage debut in a play called *Freda* on the South Pier Pavilion in Blackpool. Two years later he left school to work at Fox's, a local clothing store where he first learned the art of window dressing. He later moved to the upscale clothier Austin Reed in Manchester (often name checked on *AYBS*), where he acquired firsthand experience in arranging in-store displays. It was a skill that would stand him in good stead later on.

Years later, Jeremy Lloyd drew on his own experiences in the clothing trade, at Simpson's in Piccadilly Circus, to create a new sitcom for the BBC's *Comedy Playhouse* series. The pilot episode of *Are You Being Served* went out in 1972, and the phenomenon took off soon after.

From 1972 until 1985, Inman's character held his own in *AYBS's* microcosm of British society: London's fictional Grace Brothers department store. There was the snobbish, commanding floorwalker

Captain Peacock (Frank Thornton); the proud Mrs. Slocombe
(Mollie Sugden); cute-but-common Miss Brahms (Wendy Richard);
Jack-the-lad Mr. Lucas (Trevor Bannister); and a succession of senior
men's counter personnel beginning with the grumpy Mr. Grainger
(Arthur Brough). And Wilberforce Claybourne Humphries got the
best of them all at one time or another by employing a mix of sly
self-interest, a big heart, a keener wit and a steadfast refusal to admit
that most of his "special friends" were men. ("What makes you all
think it's a *him*?")

It was this last point that made Inman so enigmatic, especially
in later years. While *AYBS* left little doubt about Mr. Humphries'
sexuality, the actor often told interviewers that there was nothing
at all in the program to indicate the character was gay. During the
show's lengthy run, Inman found himself the subject of protest by
gay rights groups that didn't find his camp portrayal of the men's
counter assistant very helpful to the cause. As time went on, the series
gained a fanatical following in the States. As a result, Inman appeared
on several PBS pledge drives. His "out of character" mannerisms left
many American fans to wonder if the actor himself was gay.

While issues such as same-sex marriage continue to be used as
cheap grist for many a political mill today, at the height of US *AYBS*
mania in the 1990s, it struck many Americans as odd that a gay
actor would choose to remain in the closet in those "enlightened"
days, especially if he'd found fame in the role of a camp character
like Mr. Humphries. After all, hadn't the great actor Sir Ian McKellen
been out since 1988?

What many failed to realize was that for most people, the matter
of one's own sexuality is a deeply personal one, and Inman was no
exception. The actor worked to keep his personal life out of the
mainstream media until his 2005 civil partnership ceremony with
Ron Lynch, his partner of more than 30 years, made that impossible.
By that time he was already battling the hepatitis A that would
ultimately take his life.

Inman passed away in hospital on the morning of March 8, 2007 at the age of 71, depriving the world of one of the most vibrant personalities in the history of British television.

Interview originally published in
British Television No.1 | 1995

It was Comedy Playhouse executive producer David Croft who offered you the role of Are You Being Served men's counter assistant Mr. Humphries. I know it's been a while, but can you explain how that came about?

I had worked for David Croft quite a few times before. I'd played old men and funny little characters in other people's television shows. He was a man with a memory. He thought, "Oh yes, John could do that." I was literally sent a script. It was only a week's work.

But it turned out to be more than a week's work. The Christmas play you were doing in Coventry was closing on Saturday night, and this one-off AYBS show was to start filming the following Monday. Then your life got wrapped up in the tragedy at the 1972 Olympic Games, didn't it? The games that were supposed to be aired during this time were halted when several Israeli athletes were murdered in Munich by the Palestinian Black September terrorist group. The AYBS episode of Comedy Playhouse was unearthed and aired in place of the games. Fate?

They had to fill in a gap, so they used this [program]. At the end of the year, David Croft got in touch with me and said, "We're thinking of doing five more. Are you available?" We did five more to make six. They went out and were an abysmal failure because they went out

One of the most popular soaps in British history, **Coronation Street** has been airing regularly since 1960.

against *Coronation Street.* Nothing should ever be run against that. It wouldn't have a hope in hell. They ran it sometime later on a Friday night and it just rocketed off!

Is this constant waiting around for work a rough way to live?

Well, I've got plenty of work just being John Inman, as well as playing roles. I'm more of an entertainer than an actor. I don't really rely on other people's text all the time, so I've got plenty of work.

You also appear on a number of game shows like **Celebrity Squares...**

That's to sort of keep my face on the television so they don't think I'm dead.

But one gets the impression that your first love will always be the stage.

When I was 13 years old and stagestruck, I went to a school where the headmaster was stagestruck as well, and the local repertory company needed a little boy. The headmaster said, "I know the very one," and that was me. And after that, I left school and stayed with them. I did a lot of sweeping up, made a lot of tea, moved a lot of scenery.

Sounds like a glamorous life for a 13-year-old boy, but what did your family make of all this?

It was what I wanted to do, and I wasn't encouraged all the time. But it was a case of "if you can't lick 'em, join 'em" with my family, and they realized that was what I was going to do whether they liked it or not, so I got a bit of encouragement.

How does television compare to the stage?

I find television a bit lazy. I don't enjoy it as much as being on the stage. You have that audience there in front of you that you can mold and control, whereas on television you keep on waiting for lunch and coffee and dinner. Somebody puts your makeup on for you. If you have a quick change, somebody stops the tape and you do it. It's a very lazy occupation. It is for an actor, anyway. Now, with the computers, soon we'll be able to do without the actors, won't we? You'll just make an image and put it on. Television isn't for actors but for technical people because they're the ones who enjoy it.

Right now I would say that AYBS is probably the most popular British sitcom in the United States. But closing in on that top spot is Keeping Up Appearances. You appeared opposite Josephine Tewson (who plays Hyacinth's neighbor, Elizabeth) in a popular sitcom called Odd Man Out many years back, where she played your half-sister, Dorothy. Do you catch her in Keeping Up Appearances these days?

Oh yes indeed. Josephine's a good friend. I haven't seen her in quite a while. She's just opened in a production of *The Killing of Sister George.*

Also in Odd Man Out was Vivienne Johnson, better known to AYBS viewers as Mr. Grace's nurse. How did she end up in Odd Man Out?

If you get somebody you like, and you like their work, you use them again. And I knew Vivienne. So I said, "Yes, we'll have Vivienne." It's as simple as that.

Speaking of AYBS, and I'm afraid we're going to continue to speak a lot about it, how much input did you and the other actors have on the show? Were you encouraged to make suggestions?

Oh yes, everybody did that. We would have a script conference at the beginning of each episode. The scripts were pretty tight. They were very well written, so they didn't need a lot of alteration.

Apologies for living up to the crass, money-obsessed American stereotype, but we've heard an awful lot over the years about stars of wildly popular TV shows losing out on royalties. Considering how popular AYBS has become in North America, are you and the rest seeing anything in the way of royalties?

I think I might get the price of a package of cigarettes every month. Monetarily it isn't at all rewarding.

Oh dear. Have things changed at all in the UK regarding residuals since then?

No, I don't think so. It's worse, actually. They sell it and say, "There you are. There's your 4 shillings and tenpence." I think only if you own the program do you have some kind of say in what they get for its sale. They practically give stuff away. Everybody tells me at PBS that our programs are very expensive. They always claim poverty. They're constantly saying they don't have any money. I'm not calling them liars. I'm sure they don't have any money if they say they haven't.

After so many years, you'd think they'd have finally paid for that series by now.

Yeah, it can't be all that expensive because they get three showings every time they buy it.

In 1977 came the release of the AYBS movie. In an interview with Films in Review magazine, your co-star Wendy Richard (Miss Brahms) said, "I don't think the film was very good....Considering the success of the program, they could have put a bit more money into it." Is that your feeling as well?

I don't know. I don't know a lot about films. As far as I was concerned, it was a comedy knocked-out in 19 days, which was pretty quick. I think perhaps it was wasted. Maybe they should've waited and done a bigger-budget film. It was written for the stage. [In the theatrical version] there was a lot of ad-libbing. Well, from me anyway. I quite enjoyed the stage show. But we only did one season of it because it was really hard work doing it twice a night.

From 1954 to 1957, you yourself were a window dresser for the department store Austin Reed.

It was useful to me, certainly. Quite out of the blue, I happened to be doing a show about a shop. And having worked in a shop, it was useful to me knowing that at 9 o'clock in the morning you just stand about and dust because there aren't any customers. I knew how to do certain things like tying a tie without it being around somebody's neck. So all these twiddly-bits came in useful, yes. Quite strange, really.

One of the things that AYBS is still known for is the tremendous chemistry between all the members of the cast. Do you still keep in touch?

Oh yes. I talked to Trevor [Bannister, aka Mr. Lucas] yesterday. We keep in touch by telephone mainly. It's "Hello luv, how are you?" Like I saw Trevor two months ago. I was doing pantomime in Stockport and he'd been over doing pantomime close by, so he had the day off and came over for the day. He came and saw the show. And I see Wendy from time to time because she doesn't live too far from me.

There's also an Australian version of AYBS called Are You Being Served Down Under. There were about 18 episodes of that. Were you in them?

They sold the series to Australia. It's still very high in the ratings. They wanted to make their own for some reason, I don't know why. I was the only [original cast member] in it; the others were

❝ I got a little uptight because who said [Mr. Humphries] was gay, anyway? Until they see him do it across the counter, nobody knows. **❞**

Australian. I enjoyed it very much. We all had to wear name tags because I'd gotten so used to saying Mrs. Slocombe and Captain Peacock. I kept calling them the wrong names.

When AYBS premiered, members of the gay rights groups were upset over your "stereotypical" portrayal of Mr. Humphries.
I can only remember somebody saying it was a stereotype. I mean I got a little uptight because who said he was gay, anyway? Until they see him do it across the counter, nobody knows. It's never been mentioned at all.

Perhaps not, but people remember him as gay, nonetheless.
That's all right, I don't mind. They were saying it was a stereotype. But you see, if you play a lorry driver you wear a check shirt and a baseball cap and big boots and jeans, don't you? That's a stereotype. Mr. Humphries wasn't actually a stereotype. He had a nice suit, he didn't have a lilac chiffon scarf tied around his neck...

**Funny you mention suits. I don't think
I've ever seen you without a suit and tie.**

I think that all goes back to my mother. When I was a young lad, for
some reason you didn't go out of the house unless you were dressed
properly. I mean at the moment I've got a track suit on and I'm very
comfortable in it. I don't always wear a tie. It's just something that
people expect. I did a lunchtime chat show last week ... and I wore
my blazer and my tie and shirt simply because that's how everybody
expects to see me. If I go out into the street here in my track suit
with a baseball cap, I can go all over London without any trouble
at all. But if I was to go out in a navy blue suit, or a gray suit even,
collar and tie, no hat, then I'd be stopped every few minutes.

Does that get on your nerves at all?

No, not if I'm prepared for it. People are very kind. I quite like saying
"Hello" to people. I'm not a "don't interrupt me" type of person. I'll
say "Hello" if I'm not in a hurry. Nobody ever believes you might be
late for work. They don't regard it as work.

penelope keith

The Good Neighbors

To the Manor Born

PENELOPE KEITH SPECIALIZES in portraying characters who, on paper anyway, we normally would run a mile out of our way to avoid. Take the social snob Margo Leadbetter on *The Good Neighbors* (known as *The Good Life* in the UK) who, at least initially, believes her get-back-to-nature neighbors are bringing down the whole social standing of the area. As Audrey fforbes-Hamilton in *To the Manor Born*, she was a snobby, upper class woman forced to lock wits with the arriviste supermarket magnate Richard DeVere (Peter Bowles) who buys her beloved Grantleigh Manor after the death of her husband.

And yet Keith brought to these and other roles an underlying likability that offered glimmers of pathos and dignity beneath whatever life-hardened exterior she happened to be wearing. Her upper lip might've been stiff, her accent posh, but beneath it all she was human.

Penelope Hatfield was born April 2, 1940 in Sutton, Surrey, in England. Abandoned by her father as a baby, she assumed the name Keith from her mother's second husband.

Although she appeared in dozens of British television programs, including *The Avengers* and *The Pallisers*, it wasn't until *The Good Neighbors* debuted in 1975 that the actress came to the attention of America's TV viewing public. Her turn as Audrey in *To the Manor Born*, which ran from 1979-1981, cemented her popularity Stateside.

After *The Good Neighbors* ended in 1978, Keith married former police constable Rodney Timson. The pair have been together ever since.

When I reached her by phone for this interview, it was the morning after Great Britain's momentous 1997 election. John Major had been returned to obscurity and Labor Party leader Tony Blair was probably already changing the wallpaper at Number 10. Since our conversation, Keith was made a Commander of the British Empire (CBE) in 2006, and the following year reprised her role as Audrey fforbes-Hamilton in a one-off *To the Manor Born* Christmas special.

Interview originally published in
British Television No. 8 | 1997

In North America, we're watching you now in sitcoms that have to be 20 years old, at least.

That's the wonderful thing about television. The classic comedies seem to last longer than anything. If you're in the theater, it's gone that night and all you've got to show for it is a program. And I think films tend to date, apart from the great, great ones. But classic comedy seems to have a niche of its own. I now get letters from people (certainly about *The Good Neighbors*) who weren't born when I made it, who write things like, "My mother used to watch you when she was little."

What was it that convinced you that acting was for you?

It was something I always wanted to do, apparently. I don't know why because there was no history of theater or anything in my family. I was taken to the theater a lot as a child, of course. It was mainly pantomime and things like that early on. And then one of the first straight plays I remember when I was very young was a play called *The Young Elizabeth* with a marvelous actress called Mary Morris. That made a very vivid impression on me.

Initially, did you see yourself as a comedic actress?

No, and I don't see myself as that now. I've been lucky enough to play a wide range of parts, both in the theater and on television. I see myself as an actress, really, with no adjective in front of it — I hope the only adjective is good!

We're only just getting Next of Kin over here. Is that still in production?

No, we finished. We've done three series of that, and that's it.

Boy, already!?

Yes, I know. 'Tis extraordinary. It took I don't know how many years for *The Good Neighbors* to cross the water. I started doing *Next of Kin* —it must be two-and-a-half years ago. I finished that just Christmas. I suppose that's quite quick.

Here is the premise of Next of Kin: A couple adopts their grandchildren after their parents are killed in an automobile accident. Now where exactly does the humor come in?

It was a bit jarring, first of all, because people are a bit shocked that you should start a so-called comedy series with a death, and also that there should be a woman who said she didn't like the idea of small children moving in with her. But, as it's gone on, it's one of those things that everyone seems to relate to. I have letters from both ends of the age range. I remember having one from an accountant or a lawyer of some sort with a PS at the bottom. It was something to do with business and at the end it said: "PS —I've told my son and daughter to be very careful when they're driving their cars."

A prolific actress on stage and screen, Mary Morris (1915-1988) is probably best remembered in North America as the female "Number 2" in **The Prisoner** episode "Dance of the Dead," and as the biologist Madeline Dawnay in the 1961 sci-fi miniseries **A For Andromeda,** and its 1962 sequel, **The Andromeda Breakthrough.**

I think a lot of great comedy comes out of sadness when I think of the parts I've played — comedic roles. I was thinking of Sarah in *The Norman Conquests*. She was a fairly sad lady in many ways. And people seem to forget that *To the Manor Born* started with a funeral! I never got any letters then, when I threw my hat in the air at the end of the first episode: "Yippee, he's gone — the manor's all mine!" I never got a single letter that people thought it was shocking that a woman should be awful pleased when her husband died.

Both of the characters you played in The Good Neighbors and To the Manor Born were conservative and reserved. Yet there were times when they revealed themselves to be quite human, really. There was one episode of the former series, "The Wind-Break Wars," where your character, Margo Leadbetter, says something to the effect that she's always wanted to get the joke throughout her life, but never has.

I remember that one; she was quite drunk at the time. She said, "the trouble is I have no sense of humor." She was a wonderful person to play but I always said I didn't think I'd like her as a chum. But that was one of the most endearing qualities about her: the fact that she actually acknowledged she had no sense of humor. I think you'd be hard pushed to find anyone who would. I thought that was very vulnerable and a good thing to say. It was a very well written scene. She had to get a bit drunk to say it, of course.

A trilogy of plays about six characters, **The Norman Conquests** was set in different parts of the same house. Written by Alan Ayckbourn, the plays were later filmed for television in 1978.

How did you land the role of Margo on that show?

I was in three plays by Alan Ayckbourn called *The Norman Conquests*, and Felicity Kendal was in the plays as well. Richard Briers, who had done a lot of Alan Ayckbourn's work, had been sent the script for *The Good Neighbors*. He came to read it, saw Felicity and I, and thought we'd be good in the two roles. So he asked the director at the BBC to come and see us, and he heard from Alan about our work, and that's how we got it.

The only one who wasn't there right from the start was Paul Eddington.

He had done a few plays by Ayckbourn as well. But where it was sort of groundbreaking was that it was the first situation comedy that employed solely actors. Quite often the other situation comedies the BBC had done had one character who was probably a stand-up comedian or variety artist of some sort, but we had all had a classical background. I had been to the Royal Shakespeare Company, and the other three had done those classics.

And it showed.

Well, that's where we're very lucky in this country. We have this terribly wide range of work to do in a very small area, I mean physically small. You can get around. When I was doing *The Good Neighbors*, I was quite often rehearsing it during the day, and going to a play in the theater in the evening in London. And although it was terribly tiring, one job brought quite a lot to the other.

We in North America were all very saddened to learn of Paul Eddington's passing. Had you kept in contact with him since The Good Neighbors?

Yes, yes indeed. I had seen him about two months before he died when he was looking so, so ill, and I spoke to him on the phone the week before he died. And I still see his widow, Patricia. I knew he was ill for a long time. He always had a bad back and this strange skin complaint, and so we all knew and we all kept in touch with him.

Paul Eddington, who also had the title roles in **Yes, Minister** and **Yes, Prime Minister,** died from skin cancer on Nov. 4, 1995, at the age of 68.

It's interesting how these television programs grant actors a type of immortality, isn't it?

It is extraordinary, isn't it? It does give you an immortality that is very rare in any other branch of my profession.

What attracted you to the part of Audrey fforbes-Hamilton in To the Manor Born?

When we said we didn't want to do any more *Good Neighbors*, I was sent various scripts, quite a few of which were rather pale imitations of the Margo character. Meanwhile, I had met a writer who said he had a script for radio — would I do a pilot. And I did it for the radio for the BBC. I said to him afterwards, "I'm being sent rather a lot of scripts that I'm not very keen on. Would you mind if I gave this to the director I worked with on *The Good Neighbors* and see if he thinks it would make into a television series?" I thought it was such an interesting, interesting script, such a fascinating woman to play. So he said yes, rearranged it and rewrote it for television, and that's how it started.

To the Manor Born really was a ratings bonanza in Great Britain — the Number One most-watched program when it premiered in 1979. Why do you think it was so well received?

I was speaking to a Swedish journalist and she asked me the same question, and I said, "I don't know, can you tell me?" She said, "Yes, because it's a love story." Which is interesting, isn't it, because that's actually what it turned out to be.

If you spend a lot of time playing other people, is it hard to get a sense of yourself sometimes?

No, not at all. Basically I think it's the other way, because when one is an actor, examining why people you are portraying would do things, you probably get to know yourself a lot better — as long as you have your feet planted firmly on the ground. I'm very lucky. I have a family and a home and my dogs and my animals.

Animals?
Well, I've got two dogs and three cats and chickens and things like that.

I take it you live in the country.
Yes, I am in the country. I'm London born-and-bred, really, but I moved out to the country when I married because my husband worked outside London on the South Coast. I've been in the country now almost 20 years, and I couldn't go back to city life ever again. I'm a gardener, you see, at heart. That's what I like doing most in the world, really. I need the trees and my garden now.

Glad to hear somebody still has trees.
Exactly. I think, actually, if you want to put something in print, my innermost thought is, "Plant more trees." Trees are the source of life for everything. I feel strongly about that. We abuse them dreadfully.

What are your thoughts on No Job For a Lady in which you played a member of Parliament?
Oh yes, I did enjoy doing that. It was fascinating to find out the workings of the House of Commons. Funnily enough, I hadn't played a professional woman before, although I am a professional woman myself, really. Both Margo Leadbetter and Audrey fforbes-Hamilton never soiled their hands with work, ever. So it was jolly interesting to play a professional woman, and also to realize what a male club politics were in this country. I say were because it's joyful to see there's been many more women elected to Parliament.

Especially after yesterday's election.

Exactly, which is marvelous. But that was why it was called *No Job For a Lady*. I think we made three series of that in all.

You've won a number of awards over the years. What do these mean to you?

Terribly exciting and it's flattering, but in the cold light of day, do you prefer Turner to Picasso, or Rubens to Constable, or Beethoven to Mozart? I don't know how you really do a "who's best." I don't think art you define. But it is very rewarding, as long as you realize they are what they are: people's opinions. I think the hugely rewarding ones are the ones in which the public used to have to put pen to paper. That was marvelous to realize however many people actually sent a letter in the post saying they thought you were their favorite.

It would seem a hard profession in which to receive serious validation.

It is. I mean I've been around quite a long time now, and I suppose the greatest validation, the one that gives me the most joy, is when people come up to me and say, "Thank you for making us laugh."

Is it difficult to go to the store and back without being waylaid by passing admirers?

I live in a small village and I've lived here for 20 years. I'm in a very small community, so that doesn't happen. If I go into a bigger town near me, I'm liable to meet people who say, "Can I have an autograph?" One grows in the public's consciousness, certainly in this country. It's something you sort of get used to. I can blinker myself and walk down the street in London and not notice if people look at me or not. So one gets used to it.

❝ I was more the 'Barbara' in real life. If I could've kept a goat, I would've done! I think **The Good Neighbors** was preaching to the converted as far as [I] was concerned. **❞**

Is there anything on television that you enjoy or think is particularly innovative today? Have you watched something recently and said, "Ah, television is marching forward?"

"No," is the short answer. It's strange, it's such a funny medium, television. It's a bastard medium, really. It's neither theater nor film. I think it's veering now towards being totally about film. In many ways, I understand why. But it's a bit of a shame because I've seen some great performances on television that were actually given in a studio. I'd done *Private Lives* and we rehearsed it for three weeks and shot it over two-and-a-half-days. Had it been a film we'd have probably shot it for about five weeks and one wouldn't, as an actor, have had as much control over the performance. I think eventually all television will just be purely on film.

Is there a role that has really been your favorite to play so far?

No, no, not at all. It's like asking which child you like best or something. No, I don't really have a favorite. I can't think of any I haven't enjoyed, so I'm very lucky.

Has there been another actor you've enjoyed working with?

[Pause.] Oh gosh...

Another 'favorite child' question?

Yes it is. I can't really say. I've learned so much from so many people. I shall always hold Richard Briers in enormous affection because he was the person I made my first situation comedy with in *The Good Neighbors*. He was a marvelous leader in a company. He'd been a star of situation comedy before the three of us came along and he was so generous. I learned a lot from him.

I understand you have your hands full with several different organizations beyond your acting career. The Actors' Benevolent Fund, for instance.

That's my real cause. So many people in my business live very, very frugally. And then when they're older, these actors who have given their entire lives need looking after. So we have this marvel-ous organization and wonderful council.

How do you assist them?

We assist them financially. We have a nice large portfolio and we have members, usually other actors, who give so much money per year — a nominal sum of 5 pounds, and if they want to give more, they can. And then people leave us money in their wills with bequests and we have a portfolio on the stock market, and the income from that provides our beneficiaries with a small weekly income, which is disregarded by the income tax. Then we can help them with other bills, say lighting or heat, or if they need special nursing care.

Why do you think **The Good Neighbors** and a lot of the comedies you've done have endured for so long?

I think because they were so good. The BBC had this wonderful history of quality and this wonderful nucleus of very good actors we have in this country that switch around from theater to film to television. There's all that experience going on. And the writers were certainly nurtured at the BBC. I also think the situations were so incredibly strong. "Sitcom" has become rather a pejorative term. I say all the best 'coms are sitcoms. I did *Merry Wives of Windsor* recently, and some journalist said to me, "From sitcom to Shakespeare." I said, "What do you mean? *Merry Wives of Windsor* is a sitcom." And that's the thing that was so good about *The Good Neighbors*. It was in the beginning of the "let's get back to basics" movement, which was extraordinary. Also, writing those four extraordinary people. Then one had that marvelous group of actors from *To the Manor Born*, a few of whom I'm afraid are now dead. The man who played my butler, Brabinger, John Rudling, was the most stunning actor who spent most of his years in weekly and fortnightly repertory. His performance was just a wonder to watch.

Does The Good Neighbors have a particular significance for you now that you've lived in the country for so long? Have you come to appreciate some of the points made in that series?
Oh, well I did at the time. Even in London I had my own garden. I was the one who was always taking in seedlings to rehearsal and making soups and chutneys and things. I was more the "Barbara" in real life. If I could've kept a goat, I would've done! I think *The Good Neighbors* was preaching to the converted in as far as Penelope Keith was concerned.

Any goats hanging around the Keith homestead today?
No, sadly not.

Any final thoughts?
I can't think, other than to plant more trees and appreciate them. Give *trees* a chance. If you plant them, they're going to be there an awful lot longer than we are.

gorden **kaye**

'Allo, 'Allo
Come Back
Mrs. Noah

HIS IS A FACE FAMILIAR to anyone who has tuned in religiously to *Are You Being Served* or any of a number of other sitcoms produced by Great Britain's dynamic duo of comedy, Jeremy Lloyd and David Croft. But many more in North America and around the world know Gorden Kaye as René Artois, café owner and reluctant member of the French Resistance in Lloyd and Croft's World War II farce *'Allo, 'Allo.*

Born April 7, 1941 in Huddersfield, Yorkshire, Kaye received his first significant television exposure on that long-running British soap *Coronation Street* as Bernard Butler, the nephew of outspoken Elsie Tanner. Afterward, he was cast in bit parts in several popular programs including *Till Death Us Do Part, All Creatures Great and Small* and *It Ain't Half Hot Mum.* However, he gained fame the world over for his performance in *'Allo, 'Allo.* It was a performance he gave in 85 episodes from 1982 to 1992, and several stage plays. He did so again for a one-off "best of" special in 2007, *The Return of 'Allo, 'Allo.*

For this 1998 interview, I reached Kaye at home...by fax machine. The preamble to his answers reveals more about the man, I think, than anything I could write here:

"Thank you for your fax and the selection of questions you

wished to ask of me. I have tried to approach my responses in a) a truthful, and b) as interesting a way as possible. (On Sunday just gone, I was linked up to the Internet, but don't yet feel confident enough to transmit the following via e-mail.)"

Ah, those were the days.

Interview originally published in
British Television No. 10 | 1998

How do you explain the continuing popularity of 'Allo, 'Allo?

A simple answer is "because it's funny." Like all of David Croft's work, in conjunction with both Jeremy Lloyd and Jimmy Perry, it has David's magical knack of casting it with just the right chemistry. All his series tend to be set in the past so they don't "date," they come "ready dated." In 1986 we put together a stage version of the show, which toured the UK, played two long seasons at both the Prince of Wales Theatre and the London Palladium (where we hold the "house record" for a nonmusical), and visited New Zealand in 1988, and Australia in 1990 and 1992. It's the BBC's biggest selling international sitcom.

Do you recall any particularly funny moments surrounding the show's filming?

One of the things often said to us at stage doors was, "You all seem to be enjoying yourselves so much." To which the reply was, "Well, we figure if we do, you do." The outdoor location filming for the series took place in Norfolk, and indeed the good people of Swiffham got used to the 'Allo, 'Allo lot slightly disturbing their bucolic days. I suppose amongst many "funny moments" for us was in an episode where the two airmen were inside a pantomime cow costume and we had to mix them in with real cows to deceive the Germans. Carmen [Carmen Silvera who played Edith] and I were crouched behind bushes with all the beasts when one of them felt the need to answer a "call of nature." How quickly such "need" passes through a herd of 14 cows! The other time was when our rather strange policeman (he of the irritating vowel syndrome) arrived by parachute. The plan was — because he was suspended from a tree — I would crouch so that one of my waitresses could climb up and release his harness. An early take released more than the harness, and there is, somewhere in the vaults of the BBC, tape of a rather over-displayed policeman, which naturally was never broadcast. Oh, happy days.

Do you remember any trepidation on the parts of 'Allo, 'Allo producers when the idea of a comedy about the French Resistance was first suggested? Did the program receive any flack from the French?
Any trepidation of the producers would rarely be known by the actors, although David (having publicly stated that he wrote the show for me) occasionally passed on "reactions" of the type you mention if they ever arose. It's my thinking that whoever it was to whom David and Jeremy went to pitch their idea showed surprising courage in not laughing them out of his office. The French bought the show in 1989 (a 200-year anniversary of some little local historical difficulty, I gather), and transmitted it regularly. The BBC have two symposiums (symposia?) each year where they invite buyers from all over the world to see their new products. In Harrogate in 1984 a group of German buyers were ushered into the viewing booth and came out with their eyes streaming with tears of laughter. "Ve thought it was very funny — but ve vould not dare to transmit such a thing to our country!!" In 1992, Germany joined the rest of the world and proved their citizens *do* have a sense of humor!

How did you first stumble into acting? And if your career hadn't taken off the way it did, what do you think you would be doing today?

I started acting in amateur theater in Bradford, Yorkshire, won prizes in a competition judged by Alan Ayckbourn (a well-known English playwright), and at his suggestion wrote off to a regional theater in Bolton in 1968, where I was taken aboard and found myself a little over a year later in *Coronation Street*, which has been running in England since December 9, 1960 — making it one of (if not the) longest running daytime dramas in the world. If I weren't an actor, then possibly a teacher. As they say, "Those who can, do; those who can't, teach!"

Just about everything you've done in television has been comedy. Is drama something you would like to do in the future?

Actors wait to be asked. I have the feeling that even if I were in a serious role, the audience/viewers would have a smile on their faces. I'd love to play an unlikely "baddie," but our press is such that it would give that away before I uttered a word.

Lloyd and Croft used you in many of their programs: Are You Being Served and Come Back Mrs. Noah are two that come to mind. On which show did you first work with them?

My first appearance for David was in a series called *It Ain't Half Hot Mum* in 1977. This was co-written by David and Jimmy Perry. I suppose one of the odd things was that I was bidden to the location to travel by train to Aldershot. A cab would then take me to the work area. Sadly, as it was the third day of filming, they had removed the "unit" signs so that cab driver didn't know where to go. True to form and Aldershot being a large regional army zone, we found ourselves in the middle of tank maneuvers! The only people we could ask

Come Back Mrs. Noah, a one-season 1978 comedy about a British housewife accidentally launched into space while touring a spacecraft, starred **Are You Being Served's** Mollie Sugden in the title role. Naturally this led to it being dubbed "Mrs. Slocombe in Space" in some circles.

> **❝ I recall acquiring directions from a drill sergeant with me running backwards down a road as he put a platoon through its paces. ❞**

were soldiers who are not allowed to talk to members of the public. I recall acquiring directions from a drill sergeant with me running backwards down a road as he put a platoon through its paces.

What do you do in your spare time, if have spare time that is?
Yes, I do have a little spare time. I enjoy travel, gardening, watching TV and "Surfing the Net."

What are your favorite TV shows?
My favorite TV shows (comedy) are *Fawlty Towers*, *Only Fools and Horses* and, one of David and Jimmy's classics, *Dad's Army*. The funniest shows on British TV at the moment are *Frasier*, which won the 1996 British comedy award, and I like *The Larry Sanders Show*, which won that award last Saturday.

Is there anything you would like to tell the world?
Two years ago I was honored to be chosen to play "Elwood P. Dowd" in *Harvey* with Rue McClanahan as my sister. The other thing is – although I have been fortunate enough to meet Bob Hope twice, I regret never having met Jack Benny.

Rue McClanahan is perhaps best remembered as Blanche on **The Golden Girls.**

Any new TV projects on the horizon?
No TV projects visible on the horizon — it's winter here, and bad light. Who'd be an actor?

blythe duff

Taggart

WHILE IT SEEMS WE in the US have been fed a continuous diet of *Law & Order* and *CSI* for a decade or two at least, the actual honor of longest-running police drama rests with *Taggart*, a Scottish creation launched in 1983 and sporadically shown in the States by PBS stations with a hankering for the exotic. It also remains one of British television's most unusual success stories.

For 11 years Mark McManus played the dour-faced Detective Chief Inspector Jim Taggart who, with the help of a rotating roster of subordinates at the Maryhill nick, regularly hit the rain-slicked streets of Glasgow in pursuit of an endless army of murderers. Often these ne'er do wells subscribed to the Dr. Phibes school of devilish dispatch, ensuring that their victims met increasingly messy ends.

But on June 6, 1994, after losing his wife, his mother and two sisters in the span of just a few years, McManus died from pneumonia after his own years-long battle with alcoholism. [1]

For James MacPherson and Blythe Duff, who had spent several years portraying Jim Taggart's fellow detectives Mike Jardine and Jackie Reid, respectively, things didn't look good. How long could a television program last, even a long-running one, after the death of

Dr. Phibes was a homicidal organist (!) portrayed by Vincent Price in **The Abominable Dr. Phibes** and **Dr. Phibes Rises Again**, a pair of horror films in the 1970s. The character did away with his victims by increasingly complicated means, including the use of rats, locusts and a skull-crushing mask.

[1] Quinn, Thomas. *25 Years of Taggart.* Headline Publishing Group, 2007.

the actor who portrayed the title character?

The answer, it turned out, was a good long while. Since McManus' passing, characters have come and gone, yet *Taggart* remains one of Scotland's strongest television exports, with sales of £1.5 million worldwide, appearing on TV screens in some 54 countries.[2] While MacPherson left the program at the end of 2001, Duff continues her portrayal of the justice-seeking Jackie Reid.

Where *Cracker's* DS Jane Penhaligon (see page 133) remains one of British drama's most realistic, well-developed characters, Reid is much harder to get hold of, owing to *Taggart's* emphasis on plot over characterization.

Blythe Duff was born in East Kilbride, Scotland, on Nov. 25, 1962. Her determination to break into acting brought her to the nearby metropolis of Glasgow at the age of 20.

I caught up with Duff shortly before Christmas in 1997. She was newly engaged to widower and father of two Tom Forrest, her next-door neighbor and a bona fide detective sergeant with the Glasgow Criminal Investigation Department. They married on Mother's Day the following year. Forrest retired from the CID in 2003 to become a property developer.

Blythe Duff, it turned out, was every bit as cheerful as her first name implies, and among other things revealed that Great Britain may be small, but Scotland is even smaller. At the time techno rockers Garbage, fronted by Scottish singer Shirley Manson, were in the news thanks to a recent Grammy nomination.

"I know Shirley very well, actually," Duff said. "Shirley, myself and this other girl were all bridesmaids at my good friend's wedding. So I met up with Shirley then, and at that point she wasn't in Garbage. She's quite a special person, really."

Small nation, Britain.

[2] "Taggart: No Mean Feat," Mullaney, Andrea. *The Scotsman*, Dec. 5, 2007.

Interview originally published in
British Television No. 7 | 1997

Your Taggart character, Jackie Reid, began as a WPC [woman police constable] in the episode "Death Comes Softly." Clearly someone was impressed. How did your initial read-through go?

I went in for an audition and the miniscule amount of reading I had to do was like, "Do you want an ambulance, sir?" I walked off thinking, "They're never going to glean from that anything of any importance."

What happened after you moved to Glasgow?

At that point I was thinking of going to college — unfortunately I didn't get in. They kept on saying, "We want someone with more experience." Eventually, I thought, "If I keep on getting more experience, I won't have much need of the college." So I decided to go in another door.

You received your actor's union card and spent the next seven years touring the theater circuit in Scotland and London.

At the time it was a hellish nightmare. Now, looking back on it, I think, "Oh, that was the easy bit."

I understand that Scottish Television (STV) Producer Robert Love, who was the driving force behind the creation of Taggart, spotted you on stage and looked around for a good role for you. That show began in 1983 and he brought you into the series as Jackie Reid in 1990. What do you think of the character?

There's a lot about her I like. She has a lot of humor, a lot of integrity, and she's quite driven by her job. Certainly when the character of Taggart was around, I think she was at her best because he liked to put all women down in general, and she was always there to fight the corner. A lot of women seem to identify with her. But basically [the characters] are there to provide the links with the main story, and they've always been keen to say that this isn't about Taggart or Reid — it's not about their lives, their families. Occasionally we have long-lost aunties that pop up or cousins that we didn't know about, but usually they turn out to be the murderers.

But this didn't keep you from trying to create a backstory for Jackie Reid, I take it.

I remember doing a *Taggart* about four episodes in, and I had given myself my own wee diary as to how I'd come to this job as a WPC and all the rest, which I just kept to myself and thought, "I'll use it if I need to." Then all of a sudden they said, "Okay Blythe, we're going to go to Jackie Reid's flat, so we should get a photograph of you in your university gown, something of you holding your diploma." What? "Well, we always thought she'd gone to university." Well, if I'd known that, I would've played her differently!

Though pretty well steeped in its land of origin, Taggart has been aired all over the world, including North America.

I'm surprised that anybody in America can understand some of it because the accents are quite strong. It's always been something we've been very proud of, particularly Mark [McManus, who played Jim Taggart]. He fought for keeping it as Glaswegian as possible. Robert Love would come along and say, "Could you just tighten up certain bits," and Mark would go, "No, this is how I say it!" And Robert would say, "Oh, that's OK." So we don't make a lot

66 [On **Taggart**] occasionally we have long-lost aunties that pop up or cousins that we didn't know about, but usually they turn out to be the murderers. 99

of allowances for people who are not picking up on the accent, I'm afraid. It's massive in France! They particularly adored the character of Taggart. It seems to work well in the French language. The characters have a bit of an edge to them. I quite like Jackie in French, actually.

In 1994, Mark McManus passed away. I can't even begin to imagine how terrible this must've been for you and the rest of the people involved in this show. Not only did you lose a co-worker but, having lost the title star of your show, there must've been a lot of worry about whether it would even continue.
We were literally filming when Mark died. I think for a good long while people were expecting him to just pop through the door, and in a way I think that got us through it. I was very affected by his death, but because of the way the series was continuing, we had no time to think about it. Only after the event did I think, "My God, we got through that and I don't know how."

Not only was the decision made to continue the series, but to this day it retains the same name. How did that happen?

There was a big debate as to whether or not it should change, and for lots of reasons it was right that it stayed as *Taggart*. It's to remember Mark more than anything. And people would still call it *Taggart* anyway.

He was mourned by so many people...

Mark was such a character that people just adored him. His funeral was something else. People lining the streets and sending sympathy cards to you. There was a lot of pressure because you felt people wanted to tell you how much they were going to miss him. There was also a massive police presence at his funeral, we're talking high-ranking police, a sort of guard of honor. It was purely to thank him for all he did with a lot of their campaigns.

Meanwhile, viewers were also looking for some closure with the character of Jim Taggart when they tuned in to the next episode.

Within "Black Orchid," which is the [episode] that deals with Taggart's death, we're at the funeral. It was silent and I think that actually had a massive impact because there was no music, no nothing. The filming of the Taggart character's burial was three or four months after we had been to Mark's funeral, so it was quite a difficult scene to do. I think the thing is when my mother watched the first one without Mark and I phoned her and said, "What do you think?" She went, "Oh Blythe, well done, that was great. I did miss him." And I think that's exactly the way people felt. They could see what we were doing. They appreciated we were letting the audience grieve the same time we were grieving, and we all just missed him. That's why I think it's important the series continued. There's still a sense of him being there.

Did you and James MacPherson find it difficult to go on after Mark's death in terms of characterization and Taggart's storytelling framework?

Reid and Jardine were there to run the case and make sure the whole story was moving along. There wasn't a lot of time for the humorous touches, which I think was very important for my character. For a while I think the character of Jardine was trying to replace Taggart in that he was becoming very forceful, which was at odds with what he had been in the past. And then there was a new character brought in, and that was where Reid used to sit. So we all had to move up a notch and I felt as if I was slightly floundering in the middle for awhile.

Do you think part of that was due to having Jardine promoted over Reid, which certainly changed the show's dynamic?

Taggart used to go home and talk to his wife, Jean, and say, "Oh, it was hell today at work because we had to do this," and that would inform the audience and move the whole plot along. So then it ended up with James and myself and the character of Jack meeting in a pub and going, "So, what do you think about what happened today?" Everybody was still trying to hold some of the old *Taggart* around, so I think the writers have taken a wee bit of time to decide just how they're going to spread the work load.

We were lucky that Mark was the character of Taggart because he was a very giving actor, and he allowed Jardine and me to come through. Mark was the kind of person who was not particularly precious about his work, although he was very caring about it. Not like the actor who says, "I'm the star and I get this scene."

We've had time to settle down because, quite honestly, the series could've finished after people said, "Och, it's not the same without Mark." But they gave us that chance and said, "Right, it's not the same, but it's equally as watchable." The plot lines are still as strong, the production values are still as strong. I think it's only fair that we were given the chance.

craig charles & robert llewellyn

Red Dwarf

SUCH IS THE WIDTH AND breadth of British television that high- and low-brow comedy programs can be made with such quality that often they both appeal to the same audience. There are, however, rare programs that emerge from time to time that neatly blend both high- and low-brow elements so that one is left with a series that is the television equivalent of a smirking face, one eyebrow raised in self-amazement. One of these shows is the BBC's *Red Dwarf.*

First broadcast in the UK in 1988, this science-fiction farce, created by Rob Grant and Doug Naylor, quickly found an enthusiastic audience in the United States. A brief recap of its storyline reads like the overexcited utterances of a *Whose Line is it Anyway* panelist. Bottom-of-the-rung technician Dave Lister (Craig Charles) awakes from suspended animation aboard the mining spaceship Red Dwarf 3 million years in the future to find himself the last human being alive. Sure, the ship's computer, Holly, has brought back his annoying bunkmate Arnold Rimmer (Chris Barrie) in the form of an incorporeal hologram to keep him sane, but this proves of little help. Then, too, there is Cat (Danny John-Jules), a man-cat life form that evolved from Lister's pet kitty, Frankenstein; and Kryten (Robert Llewellyn), a humanoid robot with a head evocative of a novelty condom, but an intellect that frequently saves the day.

Red Dwarf appeals equally to science-fiction enthusiasts who dig its playful experimentation with sci-fi conventions such as artificial intelligence and time travel, and to Britcom fans who recognize in its character-driven laughs a not-so-distant cousin to the likes of *Are You Being Served* and other favorites.

Craig Charles has done a little bit of everything during his career, including playing professional football (yes, soccer, soccer) for his hometown team, Liverpool's Tranmere Rovers. He's also performed poetry, hosted a children's television show and, at the time of this writing, can be found playing taxi driver Lloyd Mullaney on Britain's longest-running soap, *Coronation Street.*

On the other end of the spectrum, Robert Llewellyn recently has hopped aboard one of the newest bits of media: YouTube. Under the screen name "bobbyllew" he posts clips of himself discussing everything from remedies to the crass consumerism of the holiday season to recollections of his time on *Red Dwarf.* And on his Web site, www.llew.co.uk, he is experimenting with new types of storytelling.

Since he came to producer Paul Jackson's attention portraying a robot in a staging of his own play, *Mammon, Robot Born of Woman,* at 1988's Edinburgh Festival Fringe, Llewellyn has balanced an acting career with his passion for writing. Besides appearing in episodes of such classics as *Bottom, Joking Apart* and *Alas Smith & Jones,* he has written several novels including *The Man on Platform 5* and *Brother Nature,* as well as *The Man in the Rubber Mask,* a memoir of his acting career.

When I managed to get the pair on the line in 1997, they were hanging out at Seattle PBS station KCTS, recovering from the previous night's *Red Dwarf* pledge drive.

Interview originally published in
British Television No. 9-10 | 1997

Where were each of you born?

Charles: I was born in Liverpool in the Northwest of England. [To Llewellyn] Where were you born?

Llewellyn: I was born outside a town called Northampton in the boring middle of England, raised in Oxfordshire, so I've always been out in the country, really. I'm a bit of a country boy.

C: I'm a city kid.

You two must get along like a house on fire.

C: Yeah, we do. They say opposites attract.

How did you two first get into performing?

L: It was basically the people I worked with. About 25 years ago they were getting bored with me showing off and doing silly walks and funny voices and bouncing off the walls where I worked, so they said go on the stage. I never went to university or college or anything like that. Basically with a bunch of mates we went onto a stage in a pub in East London one Saturday night and people laughed. And that's really where it started. If they hadn't laughed, I don't think I would've done it again. I was very nervous. Then I actually wrote some material. I've always written. That's where I found an outlet for my writing. It grew from there. I played 268 shows in one year.

C: Busy.

L: Yeah, very busy. And then by the late '70s I was working on television. So that's me.

C: And I started off as a poet, really. I won a thing called "The Guardian Young Writer of the Year Award" when I was 13. Chap that came second was 33! I used to do poetry on television. There was a great theater then called the Everyman, and I started off there. A chap from the BBC came down and saw me and asked me to go on a program for the BBC when I was 17. That was 15 years ago. I started off doing poetry on *Saturday Review,* and then I did a thing called *Saturday Night Live,* which is very similar to your *Saturday Night Live.* I would do a topical poem each week about events in the news. The chap who was producing that, a chap called Paul Jackson, left *Saturday Night Live* to start this new, crazy, kooky show called *Red Dwarf.* He asked me if I'd like to come across and join him, so I did.

I don't suppose you could treat us to a few lines...
C: A few lines of poetry?

Um, yes.
C: Ooh, I could tell you, but then I'd have to kill you, you know. It's a bit early in the morning for me to be romantic.

You both did some stand-up, right?
C: Yeah. I do a lot of stand-up still. I actually did three tours of England, only 28 dates at a time. That's like three months, basically, I spend on the road. The rest of the time I spend filming. What about you, Robert?

L: I don't do any, anymore. It's too scary. But I'm writing. I sit in a little shed in the middle of the country and write books most of the time, when I'm not covered in rubber.

C: [In a southern drawl] Covered in hayseed there boy!

Let's talk about the new season of Red Dwarf. Robert, in one of the episodes you're driving a T-72 tank and blowing up Jane Austen's characters.
L: It's a great day to blow out a gazebo of ladies in long dresses. It can be quite fulfilling.

C: Also the biggest explosion we've ever had on *Red Dwarf.*

There was a housing estate next-door to the site where we filmed it, so they weren't best pleased.

L: That was filmed on an army base. Normally a sort of pyrotechnic explosion like that doesn't make any noise, it's just a sort of flash, and the sound is added later. But ...boy was it loud — it knocked us all off our feet! And we were a long way away from it.

There has to be a point where you say, "I can't believe they're paying me to do this."
L: It's very often. The other side is "I can't believe I agree to do this for any amount of money!" By that time, I'm sitting in a tank that is slowly sinking in the mud, and I'm up to my waist in filthy water inside.

   C: And you think, "I'm never going to do this again unless they pay me more."

So that was a real tank?
L: It was a T-72, I believe. It was a Russian tank, the same one they used in *GoldenEye*, the James Bond movie. It had a film history, that tank. Very powerful.

   C: More famous than us!

   L: Eight gallons a mile. It uses a lot of gas!

There's a far greater emphasis in Series 7 on emotions. Rimmer's departure, Kryten's jealousy, then there's that whole Lister/Kochanski angle. Do you think there was a conscious decision to get back to the basics of storytelling?
C: It's done like a movie now, so you can actually give a more considered, emotive and polished performance. When you do it in front of a live audience, sometimes it's a bit like taking exams. You've only got a couple of chances to get it right. How do you feel about it, Robert?

L: Yeah, I think it is true. I was in on some of the discussions for the scriptwriting phase and they were certainly wanting to push for the more emotional aspect of it. They were the sort of discussions of having less curry monsters and more kissing. I think in the next series it will be a blend. They will find a balance between the two because we are going to shoot some of the next series in front of a live audience. Not as much as we used to, but certainly more than we did in Series 7. I much prefer it. It's a slightly more grown-up show, which I think it needs to be. It has to move on.

C: You need to change and adapt. If you just stand still you die. And *Red Dwarf* has always changed and diversified, you know. That's one reason it's lasted so long. If you're going to stay this kind of situation comedy with me and Rimmer on the bunk arguing and exchanging insults, it might not still be here today.

I remember reading a quote from you, Craig, where you were talking about seeing the Red Dwarf fans at a convention in America, and you said something to the effect that they all looked like they had killed their parents.

C: [Bursts out laughing.] I think you should recognize that as a joke. A very small minority of them look like sort of obsessive psychotics. And it takes all kinds. The people we've met in Seattle have been some of the straightest, most normal *Red Dwarf* fans I've ever met in my life. They're changing all the time. What you've got to realize is that people have grown up with the show and stuck with it. A lot of the younger fans are a lot more normal than the fans that were first attracted to it. I love the *Red Dwarf* fans. They're so passionate about the show. They're so loyal and faithful. They're a bit like heavy metal fans that way. Heavy metal bands never seem to have Top 10 singles but they keep going for years because people buy their albums. They're a very loyal crowd and I appreciate that and thank them for it.

Chloë Annett is playing Christine Kochanski, Lister's long-lost love. Is there anything fundamentally different about suddenly working with a woman on the show after so many years of being a strictly male cast?

C: Well, the dynamic completely changed, didn't it? It was a bit of a boy's own story, *Red Dwarf,* until Kochanski entered. Lister has smartened up his act a bit now. He's trying to get kissed on the lips, isn't he? And the Cat just wants to borrow her leg wax. It made it a bit less laddish on the set, although I can't speak for all of us. It made me a lot less laddish on the set. Some of the jokes we used to crack between ourselves are jokes I would never have made. All those went out the window, which they needed to, believe me!

L: Chloë certainly held her own with the lads; she was good fun.

C: She was one of the boys.

L: She fought long and hard — it was a tough gig for anyone to suddenly join a company that had been working together for as long as we had. We got on with her very well.

C: She's a good "gel."

Do you and Robert go to the pub together or anything outside of work?

C: We hang around sometimes. Me and Robert are writing a sitcom together at the moment.

L: We see each other quite often, really.

Any details you can talk about?

[Charles and Llewellyn together]: Nnnnnnnyyyyynnnooooo.

L: A very difficult question to answer, it keeps changing a bit. There is a very strong central idea but we keep moving it around so I don't really want to talk about it just yet. Whatever we say now, I can guarantee it won't be right. There's a lot of interest in it from the Powers That Be. It may reach the airwaves one day.

Is that Danny John-Jules' [Cat] son in "Ouroborus" as Baby Lister?

C: No, it's Danny John-Jules' brother's son.

Nervous uncle hovering closely by during the filming of those scenes?

C: Not nervous, just proud, beaming uncle. And he's a lovely kid.

L: He's a lovely little kid, yeah. His mum and dad were there as well, though, so they were keeping an eye on us to make sure we didn't drop the box [with the baby inside].

C: We didn't drop the box, we just dropped the baby a few times.

Craig, you have the most interesting hairstyle on TV, I think. Are the dreadlocks part of the costume or is that all you?

C: No, they're extensions. They were my idea, not anybody else's. They're extensions I used to have sewn in. When I was younger, I used to have similar hair to that so I thought I'd like to recreate that for the role. When we're not filming *Red Dwarf*, I have them cut out, but I have to keep them constantly when we're filming because they're stitched in, burnt in, waxed in. We used about four different processes to keep them in. Then basically they use a couple of 6-inch nails, but it's okay because I'm from Liverpool and you can bang a 6-inch nail into my head without any difficulty.

Robert, do you think working behind a mask has been more of a help or hindrance, creatively?

L: I find it's a help when I haven't got it on, when we're not doing the show. When we have to do the show it's a bloody nightmare. Spending a lot of time with Craig when we walk around the streets together, my life is very different to when I walk around the streets on my own. I mean I get recognized on my own maybe once or

66 I was in on some of the discussions for the scriptwriting phase and they were certainly wanting to push for the more emotional aspect of it. They were the sort of discussions of having less curry monsters and more kissing. 99

twice a month, usually by school kids. They come up and have worked out who I am, and I say, "Oh, you win a prize." But when I'm with Craig, everybody works it out straight away. Particularly in Seattle, we haven't been able to walk more than three paces out in the street without having people come up to us. It's a real shock to travel this far and find that everywhere we've been, every—

C: —street, every shop, every bar, restaurant.

L: We haven't really been anywhere yet where someone hasn't said [Charles & Llewellyn together]: "Hey, I love your show!"

L: It's wonderful for us. But to actually live with that day in and day out, I'm quite relieved that I don't have to. It's only an advantage for the rest of the year.

C: It drives me mad!

L: It's all part of the gig.

C: It's definitely not one of the perks. But people are generally nice, you know.

L: It's been really wonderful to get that kind of response, but occasionally you just want to buy your socks. We've bought a lot of socks in Seattle.

C: Calvin Klein. They're so expensive in England!

L: Underwear is cheap here, you see.

C: But I bought these medium ones and I think they're for a medium hippopotamus. I could live in them.

Anything either of you have always wanted to say in print?

C: I want to know why people believe that aliens — with the technology to traverse the infinite tracts of space — would finally reach Earth and crash!

L: I think I'd like to know that, too. I'd like to know how to use the e-mail on my computer. I'm so crap at e-mail.

C: I'd also like to know why abbreviation is such a long word.

Don't say that about the e-mail unless you're prepared to have 4 million fans try to show you how to use it.

C: Would that then make it "fanny mail" [fan e-mail]?

You're always on, aren't you?

L: From the minute we wake up, we hit the ground running!

stephanie cole

Waiting For God

Open All Hours

TELL MOST PEOPLE that they've got a real knack for being mistaken for older than they are and, more often than not, you'll end up dealing with hurt feelings, if not the wrong end of an indignant fist. Yet Stephanie Cole has built a lengthy, successful acting career largely on her talent for stepping into the skins of those decades older than herself and giving them a unique voice.

"I suppose I had one of those faces that looked younger as I grew older," she said in the following 1996 interview. Born Oct. 5, 1941 in Solihull, Warwickshire, she began her acting career at 17 playing a 90-year-old woman.

Whatever the source of this gift, Cole used it to its fullest in the role for which she is best known in America. As the cantankerous Bayview Retirement Village resident Diana Trent, she made the BBC's *Waiting For God* (1990-1994) a PBS staple for years after the series ended. With her partner in crime Tom Ballard (Graham Crowden), Diana waged a daily war against scheming, smarmy Bayview manager Harvey Baines (Daniel Hill), the complacency of her fellow "inmates," and a world run by younger people all too ready to dump the elderly in the nearest home.

Prior to *Waiting For God*, Cole brought other popular characters to life, including the pound-pinching Mrs. Featherstone, aka "the Black Widow," opposite David Jason and Ronnie Barker in *Open All Hours*

(1976-1985), and Betty Sillitoe in *A Bit of a Do* (1989).

Since leaving Bayview, Cole married Peter Birrel in 1995. A character actor perhaps best remembered for his role as a Draconian in the 1973 Jon Pertwee-era *Doctor Who* story arc "Frontier in Space," Birrel died of cancer in June 2004 at the age of 69.

Cole's next series, *Doc Martin*, a sitcom about a former surgeon (*Men Behaving Badly's* Martin Clunes) who moves to a small Cornish town to become a general practitioner, hit ITV four months later. At the time of this writing, the series, in which she plays the doctor's Auntie Joan, has run to three seasons and a Christmas special, and shows no signs of stopping — very much like Cole herself.

Interview originally published in
British Television No. 4 | 1996

One doesn't want to harp on age or anything, but you've only just celebrated your 54th birthday, yet your character on Waiting For God, Diana Trent, must be at least 20 years older. You have a real knack for playing older people, don't you?

I'll have to admit to having done something terrible. I was flying back from somewhere and a friend was coming to meet me in my car. He parked outside the airport where he shouldn't have parked and said to the attendant, "Listen, I'm picking up someone who is slightly disabled." And the attendant said, "OK, OK." So he came in and said, "For God's sake, use the Diana limp!" So I did. Wicked! That's the only time I've ever done anything like that.

By the sounds of it, it's a handy talent to have. Has acting been in your blood since birth?

I can't remember a time when I didn't want to act. I auditioned for the Bristol Old Vic Theatre School when I was a very plump 15-year-old, and I got in.

And Cole's not alone. The "Old Vic" has unleashed dozens of acting talents on the British-telly viewing public including Annette Crosbie (**One Foot in the Grave**), Patricia Routledge (**Keeping Up Appearances**) and Helen Baxendale (**Cold Feet**).

And surprise, surprise, you began your career at age 17 playing a 90-year-old woman. Is there a pattern here?

I suppose I had one of those faces that looked younger as I grew older, if that makes any sense. I've always got on well with people much older than myself the whole of my life, partly because I was brought up around my grandparents and my great aunt. Maybe I had an innate understanding of what it was like to be older.

How did you go about building your acting career?

When I started, our repertory system was still very much in place. You would go to a theater somewhere in England or Scotland and you'd stay there for about a year playing all sorts of different parts. That sort of thing doesn't exist very much anymore. And I got a certain amount of radio and telly, nothing very much. I made a reasonable living, but it wasn't until I was in my early 30s that television really started to discover me, as it were. I started to do lots of one-off dramas, one-off comedies.

And things really started to take off for you in the 1980s with Tenko, a dramatic series about women in a Japanese prisoner-of-war camp, in which you played Dr. Beatrice Mason.

A weekly series is very important for an actor, not only for the public to get to know you, but also for the people in your profession to get to know you as well.

What do you do when you're not acting?

I live in a very large garden flat in Hampstead. I do the usual things, no bizarre hobbies at all. I read a lot. I like taking long walks in the country. I play various musical instruments extremely badly — I will only play them when I'm on my own.

Let's talk about Diana on Waiting for God.

Diana's supposed to be about 70, and when I actually started playing her I was about 49.

Do you worry about offending older people in your audience by portraying someone so many years older than yourself?

No, I don't think so. I hope we're all sort of capable of understanding the sense of standing in the other person's moccasins. The only fear I have when I play older than myself on telly is that people won't believe it. I wasn't too worried about Diana. But when I did *Memento Mori* where I had to play Michael Hordern's sister, Michael at the time was well into his 70s, and I really was worried about that. I had a long talk with the director and it didn't worry him. I said, "OK, if it doesn't worry you then I won't let it worry me."

What are your thoughts about Michael Aitkens, who wrote Waiting for God?

It was about five years ago that we did the first series. Michael was not a new writer but comparatively new, and so back then they would take a chance on something much more than they would nowadays. Now, as I'm sure in America, we are all run by accountants who know bugger all about television, film, radio or theater. But that's just a grouse. [Laughs.]

How did the character of Diana develop?

She was a very well rounded character, even in the first series. But what [Aitkens] then did was write to my personal strengths as an actress. For example, I can handle very quick-thinking dialogue. Often after you've done a series, you get to know the characters so well, if you have to cut a bit or lengthen an episode, it's very easy if you and the writer work well together.

Graham Crowden, who plays your partner-in-crime Tom Ballard, truly was over 70 when you started on the series. What was his reaction the first time he saw you in costume?

You know, I honestly can't remember. We were filming on a very cold hillside in Oxfordshire. I suppose because we knew each other's work, you see, I don't think it came as a shock. That was the first time we'd met and the first time we'd worked together, but we had a very good time. We all did.

Do you think the series would have been as good if it had been a drama?

No, there's nothing like laughter to sugar the pill and make the message acceptable. I'm not for a second suggesting that sitcoms are polemics in deep disguise, but if you are going to do a series about the elderly and you make it a comedy, then you can inform people without them realizing what you're doing.

Michael Bilton, who played Basil "The Bayview Stallion" on the series, died in late 1993.

He was a lovely man. When you lose a colleague and a friend, it really hits you. But what can I say? The most serious things in life people do make jokes about for the very simple reason that it makes it bearable. I remember while doing *Tenko*, talking to survivors from prisoner-of-war camps, the question I would always ask was, "What do you remember most?" And invariably the answer would come back, "We remember the laughs," which is terribly astonishing when you consider what people suffered. But I think it's one of our ways of coping, isn't it?

There really is a Bayview Retirement Village, isn't there?

Sort of. What you see at the beginning of the credits is a painting of the actual home which we filmed at. And it is a rather splendid home for the elderly where you can either go in and have your own flat or you can have your own room in the main house, and there is indeed a hospice at the back. That was very much for real and we did all our filming there. However, it bears no resemblance to Bayview.

And it doesn't exactly go out of its way to advertise the fact that it's the setting for Waiting for God.

I don't think they want visitors coming there in droves.

What kind of an experience was it filming the series?

We tended to do 10 episodes per series. We would do three weeks filming [exterior scenes], five studios [interior scenes], and each studio was a week so... [does the math] it took about four months. The filming is the hardest work because you're up first thing and you work through until you lose the light. But as far as doing the studio stuff is concerned, you rehearse from 10 until 2, and then you have the afternoon off. You'll do Tuesday through Saturday, and Sunday you'll be in studio all day recording right in front of the audience. And Monday will be your day off.

So you recorded before a live audience?

That's genuine laughter you hear. The only time we wouldn't use the sound of a regular audience would be if a laugh was slightly too loud and the editor would just turn the laughter down a little bit. Apart from that, nothing is ever added on.

Check out the documentary in "The Coupling Collection" DVD box set for a detailed look at how all of this live-audience filming and editing works in Great Britain. It is the best first-hand look at the filming of a sitcom there is.

66 Are elderly people considered to be not terribly useful or interesting members of our society? This is absolute crap as far as I'm concerned. If you've had a lifetime of experience you presumably have gained a little wisdom along the way. **99**

There were five series of Waiting for God. Do you feel it ended when it needed to?

After we had done the fifth series, I didn't want to do any more. I'd loved doing it, enjoyed it hugely, but felt it was time to go. And I'd rather go with people saying, "Oh, aren't you going to do any more," than saying, "Oh dear, are you doing some more?"

What's the response to the series been like from viewers?

Absolutely enormous response. All of them saying things like, "I am just like Diana," or "I wish I was like Diana." Oddly enough from young people as well: "I wish my Gran' was like Diana," or "My Gran' is like Diana."

You told me that the way television portrays the elderly makes you very cross. Why do you think the medium does such a poor job of covering this time of life?

Are elderly people considered to be not terribly useful or interesting members of our society? This is absolute crap as far as I'm concerned. If you've had a lifetime of experience you presumably have gained a little wisdom along the way. I'm not suggesting that all old people are wise — God knows they're not. But people tend to pick up a few tips along life's path.

You do a lot of work for the charity Age Concern.

In common with everybody who's even a little in the public eye, I get asked to do a lot of things and I just sort of choose carefully. I have a brother who's schizophrenic, so I'm a patron of the National Schizophrenia Society over here. I don't know, the older I get — maybe I'm hedging my bets!

Given the choice between theater and television, which do you prefer?

If I'm absolutely honest I prefer television because every day it's completely different. I mean I've just done a run of a hit play in the West End for nine months, and I love doing it because it was the most amazing part. But of course after about six months it isn't so much the excitement of going on stage, because that didn't stop. But everybody is going home and putting their feet up at about 6 o'clock and you're going into the theater to start work. I miss my evenings at home, so I prefer telly I guess.

Have you heard very much from your American fans?

I've had lots of letters from America. That has been very, very nice indeed. When you do something you feel is quintessentially English like *Waiting For God* and then you discover it's being enjoyed hugely all over America, it's very cheering.

Anything you've always wanted to say in print?
What a wonderful chance to be given and how pathetic that I can't think of anything. I guess one thing, really. You know very often in interviews you're asked, "What would you like your epitaph to be?" And I guess I'd like my epitaph to be, "She walked her talk." That would be nice if everybody walked their talk. I think it would be a better world.

clive swift

Keeping Up
Appearances

Peak Practice

GOING ON TELEVISION week after week and telling the same joke is like using the same excuse to beg off work again and again. Sure, you may get what you want this time around, but a part of you knows that sooner or later you're going to get called on the mat for it.

That is unless the joke is the central premise upon which hangs the BBC sitcom *Keeping Up Appearances*. From 1990 to 1995, the repetitive adventures of social-climber Hyacinth Bucket ("it's pronounced *Bouquet*") took Britain and North America by storm, and continue to dominate PBS schedules Stateside to this day. Never before in the history of British TV exports has a series so polarized an audience. Sure, there are people who can take or leave *Absolutely Fabulous*, for example, but *Keeping Up Appearances* has been known to persuade some viewers to change their schedules so as not to miss an episode, while driving others grumbling from the room.

At the heart of this love-it-or-hate-it reaction is the never-changing saga of Hyacinth (Patricia Routledge), a middle-age housewife who prides herself on her pristine home and possessions, and never misses an opportunity to ingratiate herself with members of the upper crust whom she regards as her social peers. To this end, she continuously tries to avoid contact with her far more humble family members, including her senile father, her sisters Daisy (Judy Cornwell) and

Rose (Shirley Stelfox, and later, Mary Millar), and Daisy's husband, Onslow (Geoffrey Hughes). Through it all, Hyacinth's henpecked husband, Richard (Clive Swift), tries to convince her to treat her family better, yet inevitably knuckles under to whatever social-climbing scheme his wife has settled on for the day.

Richard easily is the most realistic and sympathetic character of the bunch, something that has served Clive Swift well in recent years. In addition to making regular TV appearances on PBS pledge drives around the US, he's used Richard's sympathetic appeal as a springboard for other projects, including his 2007 touring show. In addition to a few humorous stories, *Richard Bucket Overflows: An Audience With Clive Swift* gave the actor the opportunity to perform a number of songs he has written.

Born on Feb. 9, 1936, the actor was a founder member of the prestigious Royal Shakespeare Company and performed alongside such greats as Sir Ian McKellen and Sir Derek Jacobi at the University of Cambridge's ADC Theatre in the 1950s. Most recently he turned up on the Christmas 2007 episode of the new *Doctor Who:* "Voyage of the Damned."

Interview originally published in
British Television No. 9 | 1997

Have you visited the United States before?

Yes, yes indeed. I was last there a few years ago. I came to do a pledge drive in Long Island for *Keeping Up Appearances*. They had four hours of our show. I thought that would be overkill for anybody. They interviewed me live between all of the episodes and had banks of friends and relations taking the pledges behind me. They thought it was terrific. Apparently it has sold as well as any sitcom ever has throughout the world. And also we understand that the Americans want to try to make their own version of it.

How do you think that would turn out?

I'm absolutely intrigued. They were going to make a pilot of it, I think.

To Americans you appear to be the quintessential Englishman, so it came as no surprise to learn of your fondness for cricket and poetry.

Well, you're in our world enough to know that you mustn't confuse the character with the actor. I do find that people expect me to be as emollient as Richard in real life. As kind of wimpishly affable. I don't think I am that by nature, really. I think there's a lot of acting going on there.

You have to understand that we're not necessarily used to "acting" over here.

Oh come on now, you have things like *Frasier*, which is my favorite. I never miss it. And for years I used to love *Roseanne* as well.

Now let's see. You were born in Liverpool...

I got keen on acting at school, and then I was at Cambridge University with the same generation as people like Ian McKellen and Derek Jacobi and Eleanor Bron.

That's interesting because later Cambridge became known for comedy.

Yes, that's absolutely true. Of course we had the Footlights. Our lot were more legit. I don't quite know why that happened. [Suddenly remembering.] Oh, we had Peter Cook. Now he's my generation. And David Frost.

Were you a member of the Footlights?

The Cambridge University Footlights Dramatic Club alumni include everyone from **Monty Python's** John Cleese, Graham Chapman and Eric Idle to **Jeeves & Wooster's** Stephen Fry and Hugh Laurie.

No, I never was. I got stuck into the other side of things, the straight acting mold, although I've always played a lot of comic parts. I was lucky enough to get to Stratford, the Royal Shakespeare Company, throughout the sixties.

I played a lot of Shakespearian comic roles, really. Not many verse parts. They thought I couldn't handle the verse very well, which is one reason why I got myself more interested in speaking poetry. [Laughs.] I thought, "Well, you know, I'll show 'em. I'll show 'em I can do it."

I'm glad you brought us back to that. I think I read somewhere that you were actually teaching poetry at one point.

I helped to set up something called the Actors Centre here, which is really the only full-time professional training club. The headquarters is in London but we have one or two provincial branches as well now. I worked very hard on the committee for over 20 years, and that's really when I began teaching poetry speaking. It's only a little thing, professionally speaking. It's one thing to play a part, or even a verse part in a classic drama, but a lot of actors are foxed by lyric poetry, pure poetry, because there doesn't seem to be a character there. And this is something that interested me very much. I taught years ago at the London Academy of Music and Dramatic Art and a little bit at the Royal Academy of Dramatic Art — we're talking about the early '70s.

Who are your favorite poets?

There are so many, it's difficult to name because I really love language and the possibilities of language. [Interjects suddenly]: But do [your readers] know that I used to be married? I have three children by a lady who is a famous English writer, a woman called Margaret Drabble. Anyhow, in England she is extremely well known, and she's remarried a gentleman who is, again, a very well known biographer, especially of George Bernard Shaw. Maggie and I had three children but we divorced, my goodness me, about 20 years ago. All the kids are fine, thank God, and doing very well.

Did you remarry?

No. I was just thinking that's another side of me that people may not know of. I've been an actor since 1959 and I've done a hell of a lot of television over the years. It's amazing how much some of the fans know. I thought [when I was last in the US] they knew more about me and what I did than I knew about myself. [Laughs.] Some people live a little by proxy, don't they?

It sounds like you've already sampled the Internet.

No, I'm not on that. I'm just struggling with my word processor still.

If you think they know a lot about you now...

Can I ask you – I haven't surfed the Internet at all so I can't imagine what they say.

Margaret Drabble popped up briefly in headlines on this side of the Atlantic in 2003 when she published an opinion piece in the Daily Telegraph headlined "I loathe America, and what it has done to the rest of the world." To be fair, the novelist's piece condemns the Bush administration for its invasion of Iraq more than the nation's inhabitants themselves, but it still left many Americans more than a little upset.

It's an amalgam of things they've read and thought, along with pictures, discussions, everything. There are hundreds and hundreds of adoring Clive Swift groupies in North America.

I'll fly over tonight! Really?! Is that because they think that I'm like Richard Bucket, that I'm sort of a pliable guy?

I wouldn't want to approach the psychology of it, but it would have to be from that show. So, if you ever need a pick-me-up...

It is lovely, I must say. We stopped making the show in 1995 and I haven't really done any television since. I'm glad to say that actually this week I'm involved in the pilot of a new sitcom, although we don't know what will happen to it, if anything.

What's it called?

It's called *A Small Addition*. It's being made by a company called Hat Trick, who did *Drop the Dead Donkey*. Also, I don't know if you know another interesting thing — have you seen *Drop the Dead Donkey*? Well, my older brother, David Swift, plays Henry Davenport the newsreader.

Everyone seems to have worked with everyone else or be related to everyone else in British TV.

Well, England's a very small place. I started acting before my brother. He was in business, and then he married a girl who was very keen on the theater and an actress herself. And then he just took the plunge. This was about four years after me, I suppose.

What would your second career choice have been if acting hadn't worked out for you?

Do you know, it never occurred to me. I'm asked that quite a lot. I mean I got a middling kind of degree at Cambridge in English

> **Drop the Dead Donkey** (1990-1998), one of the better sitcoms to come out of the UK in the '90s, followed the insane off-camera antics of the Globelink TV news team. Best remembered for the timeliness of the news events it satirized, **Donkey** also served as a biting commentary on the then-rampant consolidation of mass media by magnates such as Rupert Murdoch and Robert Maxwell.

literature. I was so involved in acting — I played Falstaff in both parts of *Henry IV* and got very good notices. And while I was at Cambridge, Peter Hall actually offered me a job. He said, "Oh come to Stratford and be a part of the Company." This was in 1960. And so I thought, "Well, somebody's offered me a job. I better take it." I was rather impractical. My father was in business: he sold furniture. We were a Liverpool family and Dad had said, "Look, I don't want you in the business because you will ruin me in two weeks — you're such a dreamer." So I really hadn't completed anything else at all. I often wonder what the hell else I could've done. I suppose I would've tried to teach somebody something, God forbid.

You have written a couple of books, haven't you?

Yes. I was teaching in the drama schools and all of the students kept asking me, "How do you get an agent," and other kinds of things they should know, or should have been told at the drama school. Again, we're talking about 25 years ago and the only book in England was a thing called *Advice to a Player*. So I suddenly realized there was the need for a very practical thing to tell people that they had to save for their income tax, that they would be out of work, etc. And this book, *The Job of Acting*, was published and was very successful, actually. The last edition was in '85. I did three editions of it and then I frankly got fed up with the whole thing. I'm rather proud of the fact that, certainly in this country, mine was the first of its kind. It was on the reading list of all the students. Then I was asked to write a book for school leavers about the life of a professional actor, and that was called *The Performing World of the Actor*. I managed to write that while we were filming *Excalibur* in Ireland. But that's all that I've written. I prefer performing, really. I'm pleased to say that at last, after this two year gap on television, I'm going into a show here called *Peak Practice*.

Swift played Sir Hector in **Excalibur**, the 1981 cinematic retelling of the King Arthur legend, alongside Helen Mirren, Patrick Stewart and Liam Neeson.

Peak Practice (1993-2002) was a drama about a medical practice in a small fictional Derbyshire town starring Kevin Whately (**Inspector Morse**'s Sgt. Lewis) and Amanda Burton (**Silent Witness**).

We're just getting that in the States now.

I don't know the show too well myself, but this is the sixth series apparently. I'm going to have 10 episodes out of 14, playing a hypochondriac chemist who's an interfering and rather corrupt little man.

That will be a good contrast to Richard.

That's what I'm hoping. I'm delighted because it gives me a chance to get away from Richard. Although having said that, the recognition is rather wonderful. I've done a lot of theater work over the years and crept about quite anonymously. It's extraordinary to go to Spain or Belgium or Israel or New York and be recognized a good deal. It's kind of nice and sometimes a bit of a nuisance. I was in Belgium a short while ago, compering some concerts on television, kind of light classical music. And they entitled the program *Richard Goes Classic*. I just introduced the numbers. I was astounded wandering around Brussels because everyone seemed to know me! And somebody explained that *Keeping Up Appearances* at that time was on every night!

In what language?

It was Brussels, so [thinks].... I don't know. That's another interesting question because I know we're dubbed in Spain. I haven't seen it but somebody's told me. And in Poland I know what happens is — nobody's got any money — so a man reads all the dialogue of all the characters like a kind of documentary! It must be extraordinary to watch. Maybe they're improving my performance.

Could you talk a bit about Inspector Waugh?

Yes, my God, I don't know what's happened to that. [*Waugh on Crime*] was very much of its time. I'm looking up something now. I've got my CV here. Oh, 1970. It was a very simple detective series. I remember I wore a bowtie and I was a rather intellectual

> **❝** [On **Waugh on Crime**] There were us two, and there were never more than two or three other people. Most of the audience had guessed the villain in the first five minutes because it could only have been one of these two other people, unless it was one of us. **❞**

detective. Now let's see, this was for the BBC. Princess Margaret once told me — this is, what do you call it, name dropping — that it had been her favorite program. She told me that when I was at Chichester in a play once. We are talking 27 years ago. I was thrilled because it was the first leading part that I had on television. I remember I had a sidekick who was just a very average policeman, a bit like Sherlock Holmes and Dr. Watson. This sidekick policeman was absolutely thick because I demonstrated all my amazing intellectual powers of detection by saying, "What do you think happened then?" He'd say, "Oh, I don't know sir, I couldn't tell you." "Well let *me* tell you..." The thing was that I think we only did one series because there were so few in the cast. There were us two, and there were never more than two or three other people. It was only a half-hour. Most of the audience had guessed the villain in the first five minutes because it could only have been one of these two other people, unless it was one of us. It was a very strange show. I haven't got any copies of that.

It will probably resurface.

Oh please God, no!

They recently aired the Keeping Up Appearances special here the other day.

Oh really? Tell me about that because our director, Harold Snoad, did that himself. He told us he was compiling a thing. Didn't it all go out on the same night on various PBS stations?

Yes, and there were two surreal moments. They had Geoffrey Hughes (Onslow) and Judy Cornwell (Daisy) step out of character and solicit PBS pledges.

Oh my God, I didn't know about that. [Laughs.] How bizarre! Well, Harold has told me that they've asked for a second compilation. I thought that was an exciting idea for everybody to watch on the same night. I hope it got PBS a lot of money.

It really looked like you had fun taping that series. Was there a lot of joking around off-camera?

Yes, especially at the read-throughs of the new episodes. That's when we had our fun, really. Once the tape is rolling, it's too expensive to crack up and you don't get any prizes for cocking-up a take. Although obviously we're only human. There were the odd giggles.

I was just thinking: Is Richard and Hyacinth's son, Sheridan, well, real?

Oh God, I'd never thought of that. I'd always thought he was real. It had never occurred to us that he wasn't real. [Laughs.] But of course we never see him, so I had one concept of him, and no doubt Patricia had another. To Richard he was a huge disappointment and also a drain on his pocket. There's a whole storyline there, really. We suggested a Christmas special or something one year where we went to London to visit Sheridan. I think that the button was going to be that, of course, he wasn't there or we missed him or he'd moved or something. We still weren't going to see him. Roy Clarke, the writer, doesn't like anybody suggesting anything. He's so successful and so clever in a way that I suppose we should respect it. But we kept thinking of hundreds of storylines that never materialized, which is a pity.

How did they come to cast you as Richard?

I'd done a small part for Harold Snoad in something called *Lucky Jim*, based on the Kingsley Amis books quite a few years ago. They were just making a pilot and he sat me down and said, "Look, there is this script about this very snobby woman. Patricia Routledge is going to play the woman." He also added that, "She thinks it was written for her, but in fact it wasn't." But as soon as she saw it she was, "Oh, this was written for me." And I thought that was a nice kind of touch. But Harold said, "Now look, there's this part of the husband and he only has four lines or something. He just says, 'Yes dear, no dear, you're wanted on the phone,' and I don't know if you're interested."

So I just leafed through it. I was waiting to hear whether I was going to play in *School For Scandal* in Manchester, and I wanted to do that very much. Anyhow, I had to make up my mind very quickly about this pilot. I thought to myself, "Well, this is Harold Snoad who started as a boy on *Dad's Army*, and has directed several successful sitcoms. The writer is Roy Clarke, who has had *Last of the Summer Wine* going for 20 years! And this is Patricia Routledge, who I'd never worked with but I'd admired whenever I'd seen her on the stage." She hadn't done all that much television as far as I know.

I said I would do the pilot. Happily or unhappily I was turned down for the play, anyway. So thank God I didn't hang around waiting to see. We made this pilot, and when the BBC saw it they commissioned the series immediately, just five other episodes.

We shot the pilot early in the year and the rest of the series in the summer. The pilot episode was one of the first six. The fortunate thing was I'd never been a regular in a sitcom before, and we knew even while the show was going out that autumn that it was going to be a big hit. Harold Snoad, who was very experienced, had warned us that it would take time for the audience to build up, and that the BBC always made at least two or three series in order to give a show time to catch on. The audience has to get to know the characters and feel at home with them, and once they know the dramatic geography, they enjoy it more. By about the third or fourth episode, we got ratings of over 14 million.

And the whole population of Britain is...?

Over 60 million. It had taken off so quickly, that was the unusual thing. What good fortune, for me especially. This was a cut above the ordinary, really. It was just cleverer and wittier than quite a lot of them, when you see actors having to work so hard for their laughs. Not only did we manage to get the middle class and the working class thing inside one family, but it is also a family show that the kids love. A big percentage of our audience were children. A lot of adults really didn't like it very much. I mean my dentist, whenever I see him, he says, "You're not still doing that are you?" I understand his point of view because it's very simple, really. The joke is oft repeated.

Why do you think Richard married Hyacinth, anyway?

As all the journalists used to say, "Why does he stay with her?" And I'd say, "Because it's like *Tom and Jerry*. It's a joke. If he didn't stay with her, that'd be the end of our working lives." Richard didn't apparently have any family. You never saw any brothers or old ancient mothers — he has no family. And Patricia had the idea that he might've been an orphan, therefore kind of attracted to a motherly, protective figure who would look after him and see that his clothes were pressed and that he had nice food on the table. I used to think that he was a bit of a lazy sod, really. His penance was that he had to put up with her personality. Otherwise, he might've been a bit of a couch potato. He was so full of inertia that he never got into the swing of life. Without her he would've been a terrible stay-at-home. To tell you the honest truth, I'd never really thought of it. I suppose that underneath that claustrophobic possession she had of him, there would've been a homicidal maniac because of the stress. What interested me about playing it, and I hope this is noticeable at times, is how he copes. If you do have somebody like that on your back, how do you survive?

lenny henry

Chef
Three of a Kind

BACK IN THE DAYS when we were producing *British Television* magazine, I was often asked by die-hard British TV fans which star was the nicest to chat with. While one hesitates to sum up fellow human beings on the basis of a single conversation, there were a few people who instantly came to mind. *Keeping Up Appearances'* Clive Swift should come as no surprise, and *Taggart's* Blythe Duff, too, was extremely kind. But for warmth and raw enthusiasm about the acting craft, comedic actor Lenny Henry wins hands-down.

Speaking to me from the set of his BBC sitcom *Chef,* Henry expounded on his rise to the top, his flirtation with American films, and the pressures of having to be "on" all the time when sometimes you just "want to get the cocoa pops" at the local store and go home. In the magazine we ended up running his interview over the course of two issues so as not to deprive our readers of a single word.

Born Lenworth George Henry on Aug. 29, 1958, he was raised by his Jamaican immigrant parents in Dudley, in England's West Midlands. In 1976 he starred in *The Fosters*, one of the first British programs to be adapted from an American series, in this case *Good Times*. Henry played the Jimmie Walker part, which included his exclaiming Walker's classic "Dyynomiiiite!" Two years later he co-hosted the children's show *Tiswas*, until joining Tracey Ullman and an actor little-known in

North America called (confusingly enough) David Copperfield for a sketch-comedy show, *Three of a Kind*.

In the 1980s he gravitated to Great Britain's burgeoning "alternative comedy" scene, which included individuals such as Dawn French and Jennifer Saunders, Alexei Sayle, Nigel Planer, Rik Mayall, Adrian Edmonson and others. These were stand-up comics mostly who got their start at London's legendary Comedy Store, and moved on to the rival club The Comic Strip. From these humble beginnings sprang such shows as *French & Saunders*, *Absolutely Fabulous* and *The Young Ones*.

Henry was particularly taken with Dawn French. In 1984 they were married and have appeared together on television, albeit infrequently, ever since.

Starting in 1993, BBC's *Chef* introduced the actor to a whole new audience in America, with PBS stations snapping up the series about workaholic, rage-aholic chef Gareth Blackstock. At first glance it was just another place-of-work sitcom a la *Are You Being Served*. But Henry's ability to growl and lambaste those around him while simultaneously appearing caring and human made for a delightful half-hour of television. Standout performances by Caroline Lee Johnson as Blackstock's no-nonsense wife Janice and Roger Griffiths as bumbling *commis* chef Everton completed this televisual feast.

In 1999, three years after the following interview was conducted, Lenny Henry was made a Commander of the British Empire (CBE). It's not hard to imagine his infectious laughter, on receiving the honor, echoing to us from across the broad Atlantic.

Interview originally published in
British Television No. 6-7 | 1996

I understand you started out as an engineering apprentice. What happened?

Much to my mother's chagrin I decided to quit when I was 16 to go on a talent show on television. Once they told me I would get £30 to appear on television for 3 minutes, I realized that I was in the wrong job — I was getting £21 a week doing the engineering job. It was just a simple question of economics. "I'm outa here!" I hit the street running! So I was an engineering apprentice and I was going to be an engineer just like my father and everything, and it was a horrible thing. I just cut my hands to ribbons and I hated the lifting and the sawing and working with — lathes are dangerous machines! You can turn your hands down to a little point. I just decided I didn't want to do that anymore, and when I got asked to go on the talent show it seemed like the way out.

Why comedy?

I must say it was my friends. I had four very good friends called Mac, Tom, Greg and Seamus, who encouraged me to do impersonations. I think every comedian in the universe starts off impersonating other people, from Jackie Gleason to Jim Carrey to Eddie Murphy to Peter Sellers. We all impersonate the teachers in school, and I was no different. I did every Hanna-Barbera cartoon there was. I could do Yogi Bear or Scooby-Doo or the Flintstones or whatever. And it wasn't the fact that I was very good, I think it was the unusual fact that I was black and I took the trouble to learn these voices. It sort of mutated into a school thing, too, because these were not school friends, these were guys from over the park where I used to live. Suddenly they found out about it at school and I was being called on to do school concerts and stuff, so from there I just grew into this enormous ham at a very early age.

Did you have any comedic influences growing up?

Well, in the beginning there were comedians from the British end of things. Eric Morecambe and Ernie Wise, and Tommy Cooper were very big influences. Mike Yarwood the impressionist, who I used to copy. Funny thing, impressionists usually start off copying other impressionists. If Mike Yarwood did Kojak or an impression of Sammy Davis Jr., I would come in and do it on Monday when I went to school. Then, as I got a bit older, it was people like Richard Pryor and Bill Cosby.

Can you still appreciate other comedic actors?

Yes. I'm notorious in the business. If you watch *French & Saunders* or *The Young Ones* you can hear me laughing in the background because my wife was involved in those shows. I think they edit the shows to my laugh. "End it on his laugh, he's a damn good judge of where the laugh is." I'm a good audience, I love comedy. It's a more technical thing now. I kind of know what they're doing so I'm sitting there going, "Oh yeah, he's doing this for 25 minutes and then he'll hit him with this."

Were you involved with The Comic Strip comedy troupe?

I'm in two *Comic Strip* films. One is called "Oxford," where I play the funniest comedian in the world, who is also a KGB spy; and I'm also in "South Atlantic Raiders," where I play a jail warder. So yes, I went to meetings and went to parties where they all were. Of course I met Dawn there. I went to see her at The Comic Strip the very first time when it was a theater venue. The Comic Strip was a show in the West End in a disused strip parlor, and the new comedy was being shown there and everybody — Jack Nicholson and Warren Beatty — they all went to see this new comedy. Dawn was one of the founder members of it and I went there 'cause I was doing this terrible show called *OTT (Over the Top)*. I said to the producer, "We need more women writers and I'm going to find some." I saw Dawn and Jennifer [Saunders] and I just thought they were brilliant. I went to ask Dawn if she would write for the show and she said, "It takes us six months to write a sketch," and she ran off.

It's been said that your **Lenny Henry Live and Unleashed** was the first live stand-up comedy film. Is that true?

Well, I think Billy Connolly did a film...but I think I was the first one to make a feature film properly. I really enjoyed it, too. It was inspired by Richard Pryor's films of course, especially the one he did at Long Beach. That, to me, is a seminal film. It's like state-of-the-art stand-up comedy. If you want to know how to be a stand-up comedian, watch that film and weep. So it was sort of my tribute to that, really. I thought it was such a wonderful way of showing off his talents. If I could get anywhere near that, then good for me. And I think the film worked. I certainly dressed it up a bit more because I'm not Richard Pryor, so I did things like Steve Martin and Eddie Murphy at the beginning and had a little story with Robbie Coltrane as a cab driver, stuff like that.

Does the stand-up promote the TV shows or is it the other way around?

It's always been the case, hasn't it, that if you get on TV you could do more gigs and charge more money and stuff like that, but I've always worked. I've done gigs since I was 16 years old, so when I got on television it was a bonus. I sort of started off at the top of the bill in this country and then I worked my way down from there. [Laughs].

Do you prefer one over the other?

I like the spontaneity of a live performance. Even though you've rehearsed it you know you can go off on a tangent and you'll create magic in that instant, whereas television or film — film is impossible because you do something and six months later you find out whether it was funny or not. So it's problematic. At least with television you can change it day by day and rewrite it. But film, I think it's hit and miss as far as comedians are concerned.

Do you feel pressure from the public to be funny off camera as well?

No, I really don't feel like that. I know people are disappointed by that when they see you in the supermarket. But I think when you've got a screaming child and you're trying to get the right kind of cocoa pops, the last thing you want to do is 10 minutes of stand-up to an appreciative audience. You want to get the cocoa pops and get the hell outa there. But I live my life and go about my business and when it's my job to be funny (i.e., when I'm working), that's when I do it. I've got a sense of humor around the house but I don't come in with a funny hat and go, "Hey, check this out! These two guys walk into a bar..." Shut up and wash the dishes! We try to live as normal a life as possible. It's a shame, the ones that do that and succumb to that, it's tiring. There are some comedians who make me laugh when I'm in a bar with them but they're not particularly funny on stage, and it's because they've given too much of themselves off stage. You kind of need to save it up a bit.

Where do you think this talent comes from?

I don't know. I think with some people it's instinct, with some people it's intellect. I'm more of a gut-reactional performer myself, so I sort of wait for things to happen. People like Robin Williams can make it happen, whereas I react to things or, if I see something funny, I'll say it immediately. If a truth occurs to me, I'll speak it and then it becomes funny. Some of the funniest comedy is when something's immensely true. Like if there are five people on the front row wearing jumpers or cardigans and you want to have a convention for people who wear "woolens," that to me suddenly becomes a funny thing. [Pauses.] Though that's not a particularly good example.

Do you consider yourself an actor or a comedian?
I think I'm a comedy actor, really. I enjoy doing characters a lot. What's been interesting about the stand-up is I couldn't really do stand-up until I discovered who I was. I think that's the case with most comedians. I didn't realize my stand-up was going to be about me, about things I thought. I was trying to think of jokes or whatever. But the minute I thought, "Hang on a minute, I could do stand-up about my family or about being black or about being married or about having a kid, and it'll be funny because it's my point of view," I was off and running. I could write material for myself, whereas before I used to depend on six or seven writers. Having six or seven writers is great, but it's much better when you can just think of a whole routine yourself and then go out and perform it in a few days time.

You were in something called Three of a Kind. What was that about?
Three of a Kind was a sketch show I did with Tracey Ullman and a guy called David Copperfield — not *the* David Copperfield, but a British David Copperfield in the early '80s. Tracey was doing theater and I was on a program called *Tiswas*, which was a Saturday morning kid's show. The BBC decided to put us together to do this show. We weren't a team or anything but we did four episodes for BBC2 and they did very well in the ratings, so they decided to transfer us to BBC1 and gave us a bit more money. Tracey's a genius at creating characters, so it was my first encounter with someone who actually knew how to put a character together and knew what you had to do. It was a great learning curve for me. I got to work with a few good people. After that I got my own series.

Do you really have to think of a character's motivations to have a good comedic character? Take Chef's Gareth Blackstock, for instance.

It wasn't that. Tracey just thought [Cockney falsetto], "Wouldn't it be funny if there was a character that talked like this?" She'd just start doing the voice and it was like an energy, but it was also being brave enough to take a risk on a voice or a look. She'd immediately go, "Oh yeah, she's got this kind of handbag," and people would know exactly what she meant. I started to think like that. And suddenly I was doing it, too. I think it was something I always had but I just wasn't utilizing it.

With the character of Gareth, there must be more to it than that.

Oh, with Gareth it's different. I think the difference between sketch characters and characters for sitcom or film is very different indeed. Gareth is very three-dimensional and has these quirks and queerities and peccadilloes, whereas with sketch characters you want to come up with a funny voice or a funny attitude that you can get 15 jokes out of and get out of there.

Chef is a good commentary on the lone entrepreneur. He works himself to the point of exhaustion and then finds he has no time for his wife at the end of the day.

It all hits the fan in this series. We're doing a further six episodes of *Chef,* and I think there's going to be more next year. In this episode [we're filming now], it all goes horribly wrong for him and Janice because the pressures of the marriage they have where she is basically the controller and he is a controller in the kitchen but out of control in real life — it all turns nasty on him. She wants out of the relationship and he has to find a way to get her back. So the whole of this series the emotional curve is Gareth yearning for Janice and having meetings with her, trying to figure out what went wrong, and then the effect he has on all the staff. There are two new staff in this series. There is Savannah, an American girl played by Lorelei King, and there is Gustav who was in the last series, played by a man called Jeff Nuttall. And Everton's in it as well. And a new boss, which has exacerbated the situation, who is very Northern and very brash and nouveau riche, who decides he's going to cut back on staff and wants the restaurant to be slightly less sophisticated than it was. Of course Gareth hates this and is bringing work home with him all the time, and this drives Janice away. So it's a very interesting series. It's much more about emotions than it is about food. But I still think it's very funny. It works much quicker on its feet.

Is there any reason you made Gareth a chef when you were trying to come up with a new sitcom?

Well, when I was in LA making the film called *True Identity*, I used to get the papers and the magazines from England sent over to me 'cause I was homesick, and I was reading a lot of articles about the new breed of superchefs. I was reading these stories about them being complete prima donnas, sending people out of the restaurant for ordering salt before they've tasted the food and drinking the wrong wine with the wrong dish, and I just thought it was funny. The other thing that struck me as funny was that there were no black ones, and I just thought, "Why wouldn't you have a black chef in a posh restaurant?" Since the series has been out, of course, now I've discovered there are several black chefs working in very posh restaurants, they just don't get the drum beat about them so much

So Gareth Blackstock the character has done a great deal, I think, for the catering industry in Britain. It's okay to be seen as a really good chef. It's not just a service industry anymore. It's a vibrant, exciting, heroic kind of job to do. I just liked the whole uniform aspect of it — the white costumes, the very theatrical backstage/front stage element of it. The kitchen is where all the backstage shenanigans go on and the restaurant is kind of the show.

It had a lot of parallels to my life. I'm a comedian, I work very hard, I'm not at home very much. My wife is a comedian, she works very hard, she's not at home very much. When we meet, there are things we have to work out. And Dawn is a very strong personality and very well organized, and I just thought there were some parallels that could be drawn. Which is why I think the character felt easy for me to play. I mean it was very difficult for people to accept me as Gareth Blackstock. Usually I play a cheeky but anarchic, nice kind of guy, and Gareth has no interest in being liked. He has interests in being respected, and if people work for him, has interests in being obeyed unquestioningly. So for a lot of people it was like Lenny Henry fighting with one hand behind his back. Why is he playing this character who doesn't go out of his way to be liked?

What type of reception did **Chef** receive in the British press?

It did very well. The second series didn't go as well as the first. I think that sometimes happens. I thought the writing was very good, but the way it was placed in the schedule might not have been complementary. With this series we're going to get them back because the writing's much quicker on its feet and it's shot in a way that's more spontaneous, and I think I'm giving a better performance. Gareth's becoming even more rounded, if you like. The public's going to get a good treat this time around.

Had you worked with any of the cast members before?

No. Everton's been the one constant throughout, and myself and Janice. The other staff would change every two years, so it's no surprise to me that we always get two new staff or three new staff every year. I wanted this series to be slightly more ensemble. It felt like it was weighted slightly too much on Gareth in the first two series, so now the other characters have more comedic weight.

Have you written any of the material for Chef?

No. Gareth was my idea and my creation but it was really written by Peter Tilbury, who's a wonderful writer, almost like Noel Coward in his understanding of theater and farce. I just don't write that kind of stuff. When I write stand-up, it's very unsophisticated and observational, whereas this was like restoration comedy. I think one of the things we've done in this series is sort of lessened that literary aspect of it. And I feel I can rewrite this series now, so I am having some input into it.

Where are the exteriors of Le Chateau Anglais shot?

It's a place called Nether Winchendon House in Oxfordshire.

Did you do the interiors there as well?

No, that's the studio. But the hallways and the exteriors are shot at Nether Winchendon House. I think it's somewhere that gets used quite a lot actually, but we make the most fuss over it and light it beautifully.

How much cooking do you actually have to do on the set?

We have a guy called Paul Headman who is from a wonderful hotel in Birmingham, who does all the cooking and prepares all the food for us. There's very little cooking that has to happen because people have to remember their lines, and if they had to watch a soufflé rise at the same time, it would be very confusing and we would be there all night. So Paul prepares a lot of the food before we do it and it's slipped in at the last moment for maximum effect.

You were in something called Tiswas — what was that?

It was on Saturday mornings and it was a very anarchic kid's show that was watched by 54% of adults over 18. It had a very sexy woman called Sally James as presenter who used to wear very tight denim tops with low-cut bosomage, and a very anarchic guy called Chris Tarrant (who is now one of Britain's top DJs) as the main host and producer. I was like a resident comedian and character actor. That was the first place I learned to deal with live television and being spontaneous and improvisational. It was a very good training ground for me. I did three years of that every Saturday morning, and we would have to come up with stuff every week. It was quite nerve-racking. We did a grown-up version of it called *OTT*, which didn't work as well.

And what was **The Black and White Minstrel Show**?
I did a minstrel show. I was a second spot comedian.

From what I've read, it sounds like a pretty offensive concept.
You coming from America would understand. The minstrel show has racist connotations because these guys are blacking-up and singing all these old songs, but in this country *The Black and White Minstrel Show* was the most popular television show for years and years and years. And it ran at this place called the Victoria Palace Theatre in London for 21 years and broke all box office records. So it wasn't like the KKK were walking around the stage, it was an institution — and one I had to escape from. I was in this show for five years as a comedian, but the pressure of it eventually ground me down and I realized I just couldn't be involved in it anymore. I was very young, learning how to do it at the time, and it didn't occur to me for ages that maybe it was a racist thing and I shouldn't be involved. To me it was just this show on the telly that played to packed houses all the time. But I wondered why my black friends weren't coming to see me work. [Laughs.] Pretty soon after that I went to do normal shows and I realized that I was a pretty good comic, so I was cocooned in that program.

Do you think it shaped your opinion of the performing medium at all?

The thing about the *Minstrel Show* was, because it was so popular, I got to work in the best theaters in the country, and the biggest clubs, too. They didn't really mind if you weren't particularly funny as a comedian because they would see the costumes and the lights and hear all the old songs. When the comedian came on, even if he was only half funny, they didn't mind because he was going to be off the stage in 10 minutes anyway. It was that kind of show. Then I did a show with these two comedians called Cannon and Ball, similar to the Smothers Brothers. It was the first time I'd worked to an audience where they'd come to see comedy, and they roared. I loved it. They roared at all the jokes. I thought it was fantastic. I really came on as a performer in that 20-week period. These guys were great to watch. I learned so much just by observing them every night. That's where it all came together: 1980-81.

And then there was **The Fosters.**

We did 27 episodes including the Christmas show, which is a lot for this country. It was very popular, though we sort of trailed off in the second series. It was the first all-black situation comedy in this country and it was based on *Good Times.* I played the Jimmie Walker part: "Dyy-no-mite!"

Did you actually say that in the British version?

Yeah, I did. I think the writing was a bit lazy on it but it was very popular.

What was it like going from stand-up to television sketch comedy?

It was very, very difficult. You can see me learning how to act throughout that series. I'm desperately trying to figure out where to stand and why I'm standing there. It was sink or swim time, and

> **❝ There are some comedians who make me laugh when I'm in a bar with them but they're not particularly funny on stage, and it's because they've given too much of themselves off stage. You kind of need to save it up a bit. ❞**

I did all right. When I watch it now I kind of go, "My God, look at what I'm doing — I don't know what I'm doing!" But my career was sort of like that in the first five years, it was very much learning how to do things in the public eye.

You haven't always done comedy. There was this movie called Alive and Kicking...

Yeah, I played a drug dealer. *Alive and Kicking* is very close to my heart. I was reading a magazine and I read this story about a man in Scotland who formed a football team using junkies, people who wanted to kick heroin, and it became a charity. He got a little house and he was doing drug rehabilitation. The whole thing about giving up drugs is you have to find something more important than drugs that you can aspire to: it's called the higher power. In Glasgow people are mad about football, so he thought, "We'll, I'll form a football team," and the only rules about being in the football team were you must kick heroin and come to training. So he did that and it became hugely subscribed to and people really stuck to it and he started getting some results. I thought this was a wonderful story and I wanted to play this guy who did it. He was a real hard man, a drug dealer, and a kind of tough guy. I thought we should write this story, so Al Hunter (he wrote this film called *The Firm* with

Gary Oldman) wrote the script, and we shot it with Robert Young who had just directed the new John Cleese film, and Robbie Coltrane who's in *Cracker*. It was very well reviewed, very emotional.

Was that your first dramatic role?

I did a film called *Coast to Coast* 10 years ago with John Shea, who plays Lex Luthor in *The New Adventures of Superman* [the UK title for *Lois & Clark*], where we played two DJs on the run from the Mob in the North of England, and that was well received, too.

Do you think that all comedians eventually tire of the genre?

I think one of the things about comedy is that it's very hard to develop a comedy film. Comedy's about spontaneity, and when you read a funny film script, unless you're a practiced person, it's very hard to realize how funny the physical routines are going to be. With television it's much quicker to go from page to screen, whereas with movies it's like people can see big jokes and vulgar jokes but they can't see subtlety. So it's difficult, I think.

Would you like to do more in the dramatic arena?

Well, I think so, yeah. I'm developing dramatic films. I think it's much better to be the funny guy in a dramatic film than it is to be the funny guy in a funny film because what funny films have you seen lately that made you squirt milk out of your nose? Not many. You know, *Dumb & Dumber*, but it's the dumb guy, the dumb nerd genre. There used to be films like *His Girl Friday* and — what were the other films that I like — *Bringing Up Baby*. They were sophisticated and had great dialogue and a wonderful story, but it just feels like we're living in such an explosive, short-attention-span age that we don't have the time to listen to that dialogue anymore. We want quick cuts and bang bang bang and sex and shooting and explosions. I just think it's too hard to do film comedy. But I want to do it. I'd love to make a largely silent film with great physical jokes. It's one of my ambitions.

What do awards mean to an actor?

Well, when they write reviews about you they say, "The award winning..." That's what it means. It's a thrill when you get it, but it wears off. You've got to think about the next job. The other problem with it is, if you believe it, you've got to believe it when they tell you you're not very good or when you don't win the award the next year. My wife hates awards. She just thinks everybody should get a little medal and a pat on the head and given 10 grand in a brown envelope. My wife thinks that award ceremonies are silly and how can you compare Jim Carrey and Alec Baldwin? I sort of agree with her. The thrill of getting an award is great. I've got lots of friends that go, "Oh, I hate awards — do you want to see some of mine?"

The film **True Identity,** which I'd never even heard of...

Go to your local video shop.

Why do you think it did so poorly?

I remember in *Variety* that it was sort of mixed, it wasn't all cons, but I came out of it reasonably well. There were lots of factors, really. The film had been in development too long and people had lost the original spark for why they were making it. I also think the director and I were a bit inexperienced playing the big Hollywood game. I'm 37 now. I think I would handle it very differently. But at the time I was very young and naïve to assume that these people knew better than I did. Great comedians know exactly what they want to do and don't listen to anybody. I think Jim Carrey goes his own way. I think Peter Sellers went his own way. And then it became very funny because it was somebody taking a risk. I think *True Identity* was safe. It was a bit like an Eddie Murphy film. It was actually originally slated for Eddie

Murphy, but Eddie got really famous before they could tie him down for a deal. So I was in an Eddie Murphy vehicle and they were expecting me to do Eddie Murphy's things, and of course we're completely different people. Plus they made me play it as an American, which I just thought was a mistake. I kept saying at meetings, "Why can't I be English? There's lots of English actors living in New York." "No, no, no, you have to be from New York." Oh God...Not only were you working in a foreign country, you're also not speaking in your own voice. And you've got an accent coach running in saying, "No, no, no. We say Pan *Am*." God, so you know it just became a problematic thing and I knew it wasn't going to be particularly successful. It's a shame really. We had a good team and I think Charles Lane [the director] is a talented man but it just wasn't the right project for him.

Do you know if it met with a more favorable response overseas?

It seems to do well on television when it's replayed. But I came back and I formed a production company [Crucial Films] and I started making television programs because I hated that sense of not being in control and not having a great input on the script. With *Chef*, I'm at every writers meeting and I help by saying, "I don't think this is funny, I think we could get something funnier out of this exchange." I'm very active in the development of it.

Do you still travel frequently between Great Britain and the US?

Well, I was in New York a couple of weeks ago. I like New York. I wasn't mad keen on LA. You know the thing I like about LA is that it's an industry town and you can go to a bookstore and get a book about your favorite director. The thing I don't like about LA is that it's an industry town and people talk about it all the time, and even people who're pumping gas have got a treatment up their sleeve that they want to show you. It's a tricky dilemma, LA. I think the good thing is to go in and out, and when you go in, have your return ticket stapled to your forehead so people know you're leaving.

Let's turn to another of your films, Bernard and the Genie. The common consensus is that the show was pretty bad except for the moments when you're in it.
It was written by the guy who wrote *Four Weddings and a Funeral* (Richard Curtis) and it features the guy who played the Russian computer hacker in *GoldenEye*, Alan Cumming, and it also featured Rowan Atkinson, who's one of the funniest people in the world. And it also featured me!

Yes, and it sounds like as soon as you went off screen, the audience flipped to another channel.
Oh, that was very kind of them but I wish they'd watched it. It's a very funny film. The thing about [it] was that it was written for Christmas and it's a whimsy. It was written for Christmas television here — I've heard quite good reviews of it. You're bringing me down now! If people don't like it, that's fine. They can't like everything I do. Otherwise I'd be King of the World and everybody would have to give me all their money.

Who have you found it easier to work with: the BBC or ITV?
It's very difficult at the moment. I think the development process is enough to drive you insane. Never mind road rage, there should be something called development rage for artists who just can't get shit made! If you have a production company, it's like pushing water up hill trying to get things developed. I mean if I have a great idea on Monday, I'm very anxious to get it off the ground by Tuesday, and the development process seems to be about slowing it down. "Well, what about if it was a woman," you know? "Does it have to be a leather coat...couldn't it be a diamond ring? I don't know, what about

Poland? Couldn't we film in Poland, it's cheap there." And suddenly you're up against these people whose job it seems to be is to slow things down!

Is that both the Beeb and ITV?
Oh yes, definitely. It's very rare that you get something going in a short space of time these days. Everything takes a year or so. And movies take much longer. But on television, for a four-hour series, you'd be in development for two or three years.

Anything you've always wanted to say in print?
What I'd like to say is that I'm trying to slow down. I've got a wife and a child. My wife works a lot and I work a lot, but I'm trying not to work as much as I used to. I've realized that maintaining your family is much more important than trying to think of the next funny thing or trying to be in some movie or other. I've gotten much more philosophical about the whole ambition thing. You can get the big Hollywood break but you can still screw it up. I think it's more important to be happy than it is to be successful. It's nice to be successful and they probably go hand-in-hand, but I think being happy and stable is much more important. I'm really happy at the moment. I'm really enjoying my work. And this new series of *Chef* is going to rock!

geraldine somerville

Cracker
The Black
Velvet Gown

THE STREAM OF BRITISH murder mysteries that routinely aired in the US had all but stagnated by the early 1990s, with old standbys such as Inspector Morse (John Thaw) and Hercule Poirot (David Suchet) continuing to tackle each day's murders with the detached attention usually reserved for the morning crossword. People died, some cried, and by episode's end the audience was back to admiring Morse's red 1959 Mark II Jaguar gleaming smartly in the driveway.

In 1992, Granada Television's *Prime Suspect* pushed the genre in another direction, bringing us the somewhat grittier life of Detective Chief Inspector Jane Tennison (Helen Mirren), who was confronted with murders of a far more unseemly nature. Yet the stories were sometimes overshadowed by Tennison's frequent infighting with a male-dominated police force. Considering that she often was investigating some of the worst cases of murder and child abuse seen on TV screens at the time, her woe-is-me attitude over being second-guessed occasionally proved difficult to swallow.

When *Cracker* hit the US on the A&E cable channel a year or two later, it was by no means certain that anything had changed. The first installment of the Granada Television production, "The Mad Woman in the Attic," was a tad on the gritty side. Yet the formulaic mystery put before the titular "cracker," — criminal psychologist Dr. Eddie "Fitz" Fitzgerald (Robbie Coltrane) — that of an amnesiac man who may or may not be a serial killer, had a feel familiar to anyone who had tuned in to PBS's *Mystery*. However, with the next episode, "To Say I Love You," it was clear that series creator Jimmy McGovern was determined to make *Cracker* a very different type of show. It remains one of the few series to realistically portray the moral ambiguity to which we are all prone, resulting in programs that can leave the viewer mourning for the victim one moment and the victimizer the next.

Over three seasons and two one-off episodes, *Cracker* delved into people's inability to connect ("To Say I Love You"), child sexual abuse ("True Romance"), the British tabloids' propensity for rubbing salt into the wounds of tragedy survivors ("To Be a Somebody") and other issues, often with scenes that stick in the mind long after the box has been switched off. Anyone who can sit through a first-time viewing of the death of one of the main characters in "To Be a Somebody" without feeling something frankly shouldn't be walking the streets at night unsupervised.

Through it all, the reoccurring characters did something that is still rare in episodic television: they evolved. They didn't simply wince when a traumatic event from a prior episode was mentioned, their actual behaviors changed over time — none more so than those of Detective Sergeant Jane "Panhandle" Penhaligon, portrayed by Geraldine Somerville.

In the beginning, DS Penhaligon was grappling with some of the gender issues Jane Tennison knew all too well, albeit further down the career ladder. Yet after her feelings for Fitz rose to the surface, it became clear that Penhaligon wasn't just struggling to find her place in the police force, but in life itself. Over the next two years we would see her suffer the indignities of being "the other woman" in a love triangle involving Fitz and his wife (Barbara Flynn), struggle to hold her own against macho cop DS

Jimmy Beck (Lorcan Cranitch), and suffer not only the nightmare of a brutal rape, but also the trauma of being forced to work side-by-side with her rapist afterward. By the time she left the series at the end of Season 3, Penhaligon was more guarded, virtually immune to Fitz's witticisms, and a stronger person overall.

Born on May 19, 1967 in County Meath, Ireland, actress Geraldine Somerville may now be best known worldwide for her role as Harry Potter's mum, Lily, in the *Harry Potter* films (where she appeared with Robbie Coltrane), beginning in 2001. Yet for those who shared DS Penhaligon's ups and downs, she will always be Fitz's tragic "Panhandle."

When I spoke with her in 1996, her final *Cracker* episode had aired in Great Britain the previous year.

Interview originally published in
British Television No. 5 | 1996

Any idea why you were chosen for the role of DS Penhaligon on **Cracker**?

Well actually it was quite funny. The day I went for my audition, they were running late and I was doing a play at the time in London. I wasn't available to even do *Cracker* anyway, so I didn't quite see the point of me going up for the job, but it was one of those "I'll go along because they're good to me, these people." My car was parked quite far away from the studios and I think I was an hour late, and I thought, "Have I got time to run back to my car and put more money in the meter, or am I just gonna have to wait?" So I was going, "How long are they going to be...this is ridiculous...I do *not* want my car clamped and towed away!" So when I finally got into the audition, and it was about an hour and a half later, I was quite pissed. [Laughs.] I mean that was it. It was, "Oh look, she can act pissed off — she'll do." I looked suitably stern and cross and they thought, "Oooh, she's a bit scary."

Was Penhaligon as pivotal a character in the early drafts of the scripts you saw as she later turned out to be?

At the beginning of *Cracker*, the only well-rounded, three-dimensional character was Fitz. The police were very sketchily written, but very well written. I think Jimmy [McGovern] wrote them very well, but he left a lot of it up to us and our own interpretation. And I think he took a lot from what we were giving to the characters, which was lovely for us.

Does Robbie Coltrane keep his famous sense of humor under control when you're filming serious scenes?

I really love the fact that he is like that. He is one of the naturally wittiest people I've ever met. His speed of thought is very fast, to crack a joke or to do an impersonation or whatever. I think that's one of the reasons we all got through doing *Cracker*, because it was so serious and it was really difficult stuff. It was wonderful working with someone like that who could just lighten everything up — it was heavenly.

Are we seeing Coltrane's sense of humor in some of Fitz's off-hand quips throughout the show?

Not too much because I think Fitz is a much more cynical person than Robbie is. No, Robbie has a much lighter personality.

What do you think it is that raises Cracker above the more formulaic crime dramas today?

I think it's a combination of things. It came at a time where everybody had seen so many politically correct television dramas that were quite safe and certainly weren't going to be saying things which would shock or cause people to go away and really argue about them. And *Cracker* just came on the scene and I think it was beautifully written and it cut through all that. It just isn't politically correct. People do go away and do argue things and fight things through. I also think the formula for the series — the audience knowing from the very beginning who the perpetrator of the crime is, and that not being the issue, helped. It's much more concerned with the motivation — why people do these things. People are genuinely interested in that. You've got that formula combined with a very good writer. We have brilliant directors and a very determined cast. I think everybody really wanted, and needed, that project to work.

When did you know what Jimmy McGovern had in store for Penhaligon?

Certainly not in the first year, obviously. I was told of the rape storyline just as I agreed to do the second series.

Are you ever approached in the street by people convinced you are your character?

Sometimes, yeah. It's quite weird, really. People think things have happened to you. Not that they're stupid or anything like that, they just think you are that person, that character. But not a massive amount. I wouldn't think anything like they get in the soap operas. I mean they come up and say things like, "Did you kill him?" And you kind of go, "Hold on a sec, I'm an actress for Christ's sake!"

Is the fame bit hard to deal with? I mean knowing what you know now, would you avoid the high pro- file side of the business? Is it ever a drawback?

It is sometimes, yeah. You do feel a little bit invaded by it.

Like Americans calling you up for interviews?

[Laughs.] Yep, exactly. That's all fine and it hasn't particularly happened to me, thank God, but I think it's when they go into *your* family and *your* house and take photographs of you when you're not really "on duty," so to speak. That, I think, is quite dreadful.

> The final episode of Season 2 closed on a scene that found Penhaligon shoving the barrel of a pistol into her rapist's mouth, and cut to Fitz answering his phone with a distraught Penhaligon on the other end, with no clue as to whether she'd pulled the trigger.

❝ I had a script stolen from my post box in my flat: the first hour of **Cracker** 3, so I was really pissed off. But I think what they did was beat them to it. We took all of these photographs of us on the set and we leaked those to the newspapers, so we kind of pushed the story forward anyway. ❞

Does that still happen?

My God, the English paparazzi — the worst!

Had the outcome of the cliff-hanger Cracker episode "Men Should Weep" already been decided before it was filmed?

No, it wasn't. We didn't know what was going to happen.

You're kidding.

Nope, none of us knew. Jimmy would go around to us saying, "I will write the next three-hour [installment] of the series and I will get you out of this mess." That's basically what we were all told. And so he did.

I was going to ask you how on Earth they kept the secret, but I guess that explains it.

Well, they kind of didn't. I had a script stolen from my post box in my flat: the first hour of *Cracker* 3, so I was really pissed off. But I think what they did was beat them to it. We took all of these photographs of us on the set and we leaked those to the newspapers, so we kind of pushed the story forward anyway. We didn't exactly say what happened.

Do you think it was at all significant that the first time we see a firearm in Cracker is when Penhaligon pulls a pistol on her attacker?
I hadn't really thought of that, but yes.

Did you prepare your friends and family for Penhaligon's rape?
Yeah, I did absolutely tell them and everything, and I told lots of people not to watch. Of course they did anyway. My mum was very upset watching it I think, because even though she knows it's all acting, it's still kind of weird seeing your daughter...

Did you do a lot of research?
We did. We went to the police station, the same one the fictional one was based on. And we spent quite a bit of time there, which was very interesting. Then I got to know a female detective who was the same age as Penhaligon, who I used to ring up occasionally when I was confused about things or I just needed to know stuff, and she was very helpful. Then when we were doing the rape stuff, I actually just read quite a few books about it.

Were you approached by any rape charities?
I was, actually, but not specifically connected with that, I don't think.

Did audiences buy the conclusion offered by the first installment of Season 3, "Brotherly Love"?
I think people enjoyed it. It's quite a heavy story to come in on a third series with, but I think it's very good.

Do you have a favorite episode?

Yeah, I do. It's from the first series. I like "To Say I Love You." I think it was beautifully directed and beautifully acted. It was really on the line of being very funny and very nasty and very, very sad.

And so it did. "Lucky White Ghost," set in Hong Kong, was a one-off installment that aired in the UK in 1996.

Any plans to make a fourth season?

We're almost 99.9% not doing another series. There is a Christmas special which I unfortunately can't do because I'm committed to work at the National, but that is going ahead in Hong Kong, I think.

Do you have a feeling that Jimmy McGovern has a plan to bump off Penhaligon?

[Laughs.] I don't know. I hope he does. I think it would be kind of stretching people's imaginations in a way slightly.

It is a police force...

Yes, it's a police force, but bear in mind Penhaligon's already been raped quite violently, two of her coworkers have been murdered. I think it would be slightly awful if she were bumped off or killed herself or something like that.

What are your impressions of Robert Carlyle, the psycho in "To Be a Somebody"?

Fantastic. He's a brilliant actor. Have you seen him in *Trainspotting*? He's wonderful in that as well. And he's actually from Scotland. He has a broad Glaswegian accent and he spoke in a Liverpool accent throughout the whole of filming. When he started speaking in his normal voice I just couldn't get a grip on it at all. I was thinking, "Stop putting on that funny accent."

And Robbie Coltrane?

Yes, well Robbie's a great friend and I've loved working with him, and I'm really sad we're not doing another series together. He's so talented. To work with somebody like that — he's taught me so much.

What first attracted you to the acting life?

I enjoy it. I feel very fulfilled from doing it. I like the excitement, the challenge — I like challenges in my life. I find that I can easily stagnate if things are too "Steady Eddie." I think in the acting profession you can't really ever sit back and relax. You're always pushing back the barriers trying to move forward. I might not necessarily like it, but I certainly thrive on it.

Do you become emotionally involved with your work?

I think I do. I really don't understand how you can be an actor or actress and not. If you're really feeling what that person feels it's going to affect you, isn't it? I don't go around in character all the time, but I think when you go home at night, it's not always easy to shake it off.

the '00s & beyond

beryl &sue vertue

Coupling
Jekyll
Mr. Bean

GREAT DYNASTIES OF ACTORS are rare, but they do happen. You have your Barrymores, of course, and your Redgraves. But there also are great dynasties of talent behind the camera, though seldom do they enjoy the same limelight. In the world of British television, one of the most intriguing dynasties is that of Beryl Vertue and her daughter, Sue.

The story of Beryl Vertue's career reads as a highlights reel of the genre itself. Her past accomplishments include acting as agent for Eric Sykes and Spike Milligan of *Goon Show* fame, Tony Hancock of *Hancock's Half Hour*, and Frankie Howerd of *That Was the Week That Was* and *Up Pompeii*, among others. However, it was the formation of Associated London Scripts with school friend Alan Simpson (co-creator of the sitcom *Steptoe & Son*), Ray Galton and Johnny Speight that had the greatest impact on American audiences.

In 1967, Australian-born entertainment mogul Robert Stigwood acquired ALS and appointed Vertue deputy chairman of his Robert Stigwood Organization. There she proceeded to pioneer the concept of reselling successful British television formats to other markets. The truth is there would be no *All in the Family* or *Sanford & Son* if she hadn't sold American producers on *Till Death Us Do Part* and *Steptoe & Son*, respectively. Since then, North America has snapped up several shows from across the pond, though seldom do networks publicize the fact.

Never one to rest on her laurels, Beryl Vertue produced a number of television movies in America, and in the 1980s formed Hartswood Films, an independent TV production company that has significantly pushed the medium forward with its offerings for the BBC, ITV and Channel 4. While the company has produced a number of successful series, including *Men Behaving Badly* and *Is it Legal*, it was the launch of the BBC comedic masterpiece *Coupling* in 2000 that cemented the company's reputation with British television viewers worldwide.

Initially conceived as a response to the UK popularity of the American sitcom *Friends*, *Coupling* quickly differentiated itself with a level of invention and comedic writing never before seen on either side of the Atlantic. When it came to examining the differences between the sexes and the absurdity of human existence, *Coupling* took no prisoners. Detailing the adventures of six London thirtysomethings, it played fast and loose with episode timelines and multiple viewpoints, delivering laughs — real laughs — based on character personalities rather than the interchangeable one-liners so common in sitcoms today. In America, the show bounced around PBS for a while before finding a home on the BBC America cable channel.

Coupling wasn't just another Hartswood offering — it was a family affair. Written by Steven Moffat, who started his television career writing the criminally-under-aired young adult program *Press Gang*, *Coupling* was based on the relationship of Moffat and his wife, Sue Vertue, who produced the program. A year before *Coupling's* debut, Beryl Vertue's daughter had joined Hartswood fresh from the Tiger Aspect Productions television company, where she had produced two PBS mainstays: *The Vicar of Dibley* and *Mr. Bean.*

Another daughter, Debbie, joined Hartswood in 1993, coordinating production on *Is It Legal* and serving as production manager for *Men Behaving Badly*, suggesting that the Vertue dynasty is growing further still. Debbie has since become general manager for Hartswood.

In 2007, Moffat and mother-in-law Beryl Vertue unleashed *Jekyll*, a six-episode series starring *Cold Feet's* James Nesbitt as the descendant of the legendary man/monster, whose performance earned him a Golden Globe nomination for Best Actor. Once again Moffat's writing balanced cutting-edge wit with thought-provoking character insights to bring Robert Louis Stevenson's classic tale into the modern age. That the series starred arguably the greatest television actor of his time certainly didn't hurt matters.

At the time I spoke with the Vertues, *Jekyll* had just been released on DVD in America and Steven Moffat was writing regularly for the BBC's new *Doctor Who* series.

Exclusive interview **10.17 | 2007**

Jekyll wrapped up on the BBC America cable channel here in the States fairly recently, and now it's already on DVD. That's a pretty fast turnaround.

Beryl: *Jekyll* finished production Christmas. It took quite a while preparing it. There were two directors for that, otherwise your post-production takes forever with one director.

There are some great extras on the DVD, including some rather informative audio commentaries.

B: People like the extras, I think. They are really interested in programming, but you don't want to tell them too much or the magic goes.

Sue: It's slightly surprising how many people do watch them. Steven and I were recognized at an opera in Greece, in a village square.

Sue, you've been the producer and associate producer on a number of television comedy hits, ranging from Mr. Bean to The Vicar of Dibley and Coupling. What, to your mind, are the essential elements of a successful comedy?

S: I think most comedies that work have some sort of "connection" with the audience. However extreme a comedy might be, it's good if the viewer thinks, "Oh, I know someone a bit like that." Even with *Mr. Bean*, which obviously is a very extreme physical comedy, people came up to me and said they "were a bit of a Mr. Bean themselves." British humor seems to be a longer game than American humor, but then perhaps that's partly to do with us having a longer half-hour to play with — a BBC half-hour is 29 minutes. We tend to have less one-liners unless we've built that joke up throughout the rest of the program. The rhythm tends to be slower in the UK as well, but that may well be to do with the difference in accents and how we speak. For example, in a bar in the US people tend to say, "Gimme a beer" and it sounds absolutely fine, whereas if we said that in the UK it would sound rude, so we say, "Could I have a beer, please" — already double the amount of words!

B: Our scenes are longer, which is the way we shoot it. In America, when I went to the recordings of a comedy, we had hardly done a little scene, then it stops and on with the next one. [American] cameras are a fixed setup, therefore you have to shoot it in a certain way. Then you stop and do it in another direction. Then you've got adverts coming in every second.

S: We have another 7 minutes to play with, basically.

B: Having 59 minutes of screen time makes a big difference in drama. Quite often writers like writing drama for ITV because it's less: 48 minutes. When you write an hour of drama in the UK, it can affect the kind of story you're telling. *Jekyll* we made shorter anyway — it went out in a 50-minute slot. But then we had to cut it when it went out on BBC America. It's quite a hard one to cut because it's quite dense in its plotting; something they could've cut in a previous episode really would've mattered. That was something we learned about the cutting: It can be quite brutal because of the commercials.

How does making television in Great Britain differ from practicing the same craft in America?

S: British and American television are both very good but very different. We don't have the system of the team writing [that American television has], mostly because we don't have the money here. You have the writer writing the whole series, so they play more with it in their heads.

B: Also in the UK, actors have never been thought badly of if they did film and did television and then went into theater. Everybody thought that was a normal thing. Judi Dench, she does things like that. Helen Mirren. Jim Broadbent. What they go from is one good role to another, not so fussed by medium. In America I remember if you were in film, you didn't do television.

It just so happened that I worked with Jack Lemon and Kirk Douglas. They were very successful film stars but they liked the roles I was offering, particularly Jack Lemon with *The Entertainer* [1976]. I remember he personally took me to his office to meet with his agents, four of them all sitting around, and said to them, "I just wanted to say guys, I really want to do this."

S: An agent's nightmare.

B: Now much of that's changed in America. You have got stars like Glenn Close doing television. I think what is different is our runs are very much shorter, so there's not such a palaver of signing people up for seven years when just doing a pilot. You get a certain kind of actor who goes in knowing that. Hugh Laurie is a good example of a British actor who's done a brilliant job.

S: We don't pay enough to sign them up for seven years.

B: When we're doing a series or something, we do take an

option on people, but really not much more than for another series. Somehow if people really want to do it, it works out.

Coupling remains one of the wittiest, most inventive sitcoms seen anywhere. Yet when NBC tried to remake it for an American audience in 2003, it just didn't seem to take hold. Why do you think that is?
B: It suffered greatly from interference.

S: I think there are many reasons so we'll probably never know, but I think one of them was that there was never really a proper handover from Steven to the US show runner. Not the show runner's fault but the first time they met was after the second pilot had been made, which means he was working in a bit of a void. It's not just the scripts that make something work, it's what's not in the scripts. It's what Steven knew about the characters, what made them tick, what he'd tried and hadn't worked. All that is invaluable for a show — it is the "soul" of the show and it's not written down anywhere.

Yet it's been sold successfully elsewhere, hasn't it?
B: It's interesting you get something like *Coupling* that's been sold all over the world in its original form, and in some countries the format has been sold so they're doing it in their own language, as in Greece and Romania, for example. They used the same camera shots and everything. Of course we can't understand a word.

This year hasn't been a good one for the BBC. It's been told that it won't be getting as much money as it would like to fund its operations.
B: There's a lot of cost cutting going on at the moment.

S: And the BBC is going to lose about 1,700 people in the next 18 months.

One of the Vertues' recent successes is the sitcom **Coupling**: (sitting, l to r) Ben Miles, Gina Bellman, Jack Davenport, Sarah Alexander. (Standing, l to r): Richard Coyle, Kate Isitt.

66 It's not just the scripts that make something work, it's what's not in the scripts. It's what Steven knew about the characters, what made them tick. 99

66 In the UK, actors have never been thought badly of if they did film and did television and then went into theater. Everybody thought that was a normal thing. Judi Dench, she does things like that. Helen Mirren. Jim Broadbent. What they go from is one good role to another, not so fussed by medium. 99

How is this all affecting your own output?

S: We can still work with the BBC. The majority of our money would come from the license money of the BBC, and then we find money elsewhere — advances from DVD sales, things like that. By the time we go into making a program, we'd be fully funded. We can make six or 12 [episodes] and we can make a living out of it. But it may have quite a knock-on effect on what you can make.

B: One of the reasons why, back in the '70s, I went to produce television in America was because you couldn't do it in the UK. There was no such thing as an independent producer, you either worked for the BBC or ITV. Now it's a different kettle of fish.

S: But there is a danger that [BBC] license fees are dropping and money's getting tighter, and I think we do have a problem.

B: The budgets that are being offered by broadcasters are dropping: ITV because the advertising is affecting them, the BBC because the license fee is lower. It's just dropping all around. It's all sort of doable but it takes more time and you have somewhat more fragmentation in financing the budget. Because we now own the rights, at least it's in one's hands to do that.

Meanwhile, Hartswood Films continues to produce new programs, and Sue, your husband now is writing for arguably the most internationally famous British TV series in history: Doctor Who.

S: I've got a 5-year-old who is already trying to come up with ideas for *Doctor Who* stories.

And the good Doctor has recently found himself with a new traveling companion: comedic actress Catherine Tate.

S: I think she's funny and certainly a match for the Doctor.

B: *Doctor Who*'s been a huge success over here — 7 o'clock family viewing. Saturday nights are *X Factor, Strictly Come Dancing, Doctor Who* and rugby at the moment. We have quite a number of documentaries in prime time, too — it's very different television, really. And long may it continue.

bibliography

Despite the rich history of British television's golden age, few books have been written on the programs that made such an impact on so many people's lives. Still, there are a few that are welcome additions to any British TV fan's library. Most are available used on Amazon.com or elsewhere online. And to find more information about British television online, don't forget to check out the *30 Years of British Television* Web site, which includes a related blog and links: www.britishtvbook.com

British Television Itself

Cornell, Paul, and Martin Day and Keith Topping. *Guinness Book of Classic British TV.* Guinness World Records Limited. 1996. **»** Easily the best written, most insightful book about the medium I've come across.

'Allo, 'Allo

Fairfax, Rene, and John Haselden. *'Allo, 'Allo: The Complete War Diaries of René Artois.* BBC Books. 1997. **»**Contains much of the first few seasons of this Britcom in diary form.

Are You Being Served

Lloyd, Jeremy. *The Are You Being Served Stories.* KQED Books. 1997. **»**"Camping In" and other episodes are presented in a short story format by *AYBS* co-creator Lloyd.

Richard, Wendy. *My Life Story.* Simon & Schuster UK. 2001. **»**While thin on *AYBS* anecdotes, this autobiography sheds some welcome light on one of British television's most-loved actors.

Rigelsford, Adrian. *Are You Being Served: The Inside Story of Britain's Funniest—And Public Television's Favorite—Comedy Series.* KQED Books. 1995. **»**Though not as detailed as the volume below, this one's still a nice addition for the *AYBS* completist.

Webber, Richard. *Are You Being Served: A Celebration of 25 Years.* Welcome Rain. 1998. **»**A photo-packed episode guide and history of the show.

Chef

Margolis, Jonathan. *Lenny Henry.* Orion Mass Market Paperback. 1996. **»**The only thing approaching a biography of *Chef's* star.

Wilmut, Roger, and Peter Rosengard. *Didn't You Kill My Mother-In-Law?* Heinemann. 1989. **»**A well-researched history of Great Britain's "alternative comedy" scene, from French & Saunders to Lenny Henry and more.

Cracker

Crace, John. *Cracker: The Truth Behind the Fiction.* Boxtree. 1995. **»**A few black and white photos and some interesting insights, but contains too much about real serial-killer cases for a 128 book. Only covers the first season.

The Good Neighbors

Eddington, Paul. *So Far, So Good.* Hodder & Stoughton. 1995. **»**Autobiography of the fine actor who played Jerry Leadbetter.

Sparks, Christine, and John Esmonde and Bob Larbey. *More of the Good Life*. Penguin. 1977. »Novelization. (Note that the UK title of *The Good Neighbors* is *The Good Life*.)

Keeping Up Appearances

Clarke, Roy, and Jonathan Rice. *Hyacinth Bucket's Book of Etiquette for the Socially Less Fortunate*. BBC Publications. 1994. »For those who love *KUA*'s "joke oft repeated," this isn't a bad way to pass a drizzly afternoon.

Clarke, Roy, and Jonathan Rice. *Hyacinth Bucket's Hectic Social Calendar*. BBC Books. 1997. »A fun romp through Mrs. Bucket's mind in the form of her diary. A chuckle for *KUA* fans, but a bit tiring for anyone else.

Monty Python

There have been dozens and dozens of books penned on the subject of this comedy troupe since they surfaced more than 30 years ago. Here are just a few:

Chapman, Graham, and Michael Palin, etc. *The Pythons: Autobiography by the Pythons*.

Thomas Dunne Books. 2003. »A photo-packed, fairly complete history of Python in their own words. Though only 368 pages, a real lap-breaker of a book.

Chapman, Graham, and Eric Idle, etc. *The Complete Monty Python's Flying Circus; All the Words Volumes One and Two*. Pantheon. 1989. » Every line from nearly every episode of *Monty Python's Flying Circus*. A must for any fan.

Red Dwarf

Dessau, Bruce. *Official Red Dwarf Companion*. Titan Books. 1992. »Only 96 pages but some good photos.

Naylor, Grant. *Red Dwarf Omnibus*. Penguin. 1992. »The first two novels in the *Red Dwarf* series by show creators Rob Grant and Doug Naylor — almost as much fun as watching the show.

Rumpole Of The Bailey

The only way to experience Horace Rumpole in book form is to read Rumpole's adventures by creator John Mortimer. Many of the early short stories are collected in three omnibus editions (*The*

First Rumpole Omnibus, etc.) from Penguin.

Taggart

Quinn, Thomas. *25 Years of Taggart*. Headline Book Publishing. 2007. » Good photos from *Taggart*'s lengthy history as well as frank discussion of the title star's alcoholism and its impact on the series.

To the Manor Born

Spence, Peter. *To the Manor Born*. Books one and two. Arrow Books. 1979, 1980. » Hard to find, these novelizations fetch some steep prices on Amazon.com these days. Tip: You can save a few dollars by ordering them on Amazon. co.uk instead.

Waiting For God

Ableman, Paul. *Waiting For God*. BBC Publications. 1995. »Novelization of several episodes in the series.

index

Printed in the United States
219863BV00002B/6/P

9 781593 931438